YOU AND YOUR SOLICITOR
By
Laurence Kingsley

Foreword by Martin Mears, Past President of the Law Society

"All professions are conspiracies against the laity" from The Doctors Dilemma, by George Bernard Shaw.

This book is dedicated to solicitors, who are purveyors of legal services to society, and of course their clients.

Straightforward Publishing
38 Cromwell Road
London E17 9JN

© Laurence Kingsley 1999

All rights reserved. No part of this publication may be reproduced, in a retrieval system or transmitted by any means, electronic or mechanical, photocopying or otherwise, without the prior permission of the copyright owner.

ISBN 1899924 28 0

Printed in England by The Book Company, Ipswich

Cover Photograph by Laurence Kingsley

Cover design by Straightforward Graphics

Whilst every effort has been made to ensure that the information in this book is accurate at the time of going to print, the author and the publisher cannot accept liability for any errors or omissions or for any material changes in the published field.

CONTENTS

PART I – THE SOLICITOR

Introduction	1
(a) Why Should You Have a Solicitor?	3
(b) The Solicitor's Qualification and Experience	5
(c) What Only Solicitors May Do	6
(d) Accounts Regulations Governing Solicitors	8
(e) Professional Indemnity Insurance and the Compensation Fund	16
(f) Conveyancing and Mortgages	20
(g) How should you select your solicitor?	23

PART II – YOU WITH YOUR SOLICITOR

(a) The Retainer	26
(b) The Fees	28
(c) Legal Aid, Conditional Fee Agreements and Legal Expenses Insurance	34
(d) What should you expect from your solicitor? What may he do and not do for you?	37

(e)	Instructing Your Solicitor; What your solicitor should expect from you.	41
(f)	Client care	45
(g)	Confidentiality	48
(h)	Conflicts of Interest	52
(i)	Relationship with other solicitors	55
(j)	Undertakings	57
(k)	Litigation and Advocacy: Misleading the Court	60
(l)	Witnesses	63
(m)	Commission and Interest	64
(n)	Changing your solicitor	68
(o)	Termination of retainer; Lien	69

PART III – YOU AGAINST YOUR SOLICITOR

(a)	What remedies have you against your solicitor?	72
(b)	Complaint to the OSS.	73
(c)	The Legal Services Ombudsman	79
(d)	Delay and Negligence	81
(e)	Remuneration Certificates and Detailed Assessments of Costs	86

(f)	Certificate as to Interest	96
(g)	Financial Investigation	97
(h)	The Solicitors' Disciplinary Tribunal	98
(i)	Applications to High Court	101
(j)	Interventions	102

Appendix 1: Solicitors Act 1974	110
Appendix 2: Solicitors' Accounts Rules 1991	143
Appendix3: Rules of the Supreme Court	154
Appendix4: Draft Claim in the case between Vic Seixas and Emm Bezell & Lawless	157

Foreword

For most people the law is still an area of mystery and this is true even for those who employ a solicitor from time to time.

Laurence Kingsley's book serves as an excellent demystifier. It tells clients (actual or prospective) exactly what their solicitor is for and what he or she does. The book will also assist solicitors themselves since it is much easier to act for clients who are well informed about what they can expect. The passages on Legal Aid, conditional fee agreements and legal expenses insurance are particularly useful. For most people, of course, their contact with a solicitor is most likely to occur via a conveyancing transaction and the book describes the professional framework within which conveyancing solicitors operate.

How should you choose a solicitor? The book makes various suggestions. None of these is guaranteed to produce the right person for the right job. Personal recommendation probably remains the best selection process. While lawyers as a whole are never popular, research has shown that the great majority of clients are satisfied with their own solicitor.

And in the event of dissatisfaction? The book contains a section on the methods of redress available to clients unhappy with their solicitor's services. Here it is fair to say that most solicitors are now well aware that any dissatisfied client represents failure and they will do their best to resolve a complaint amicably.

There is, so far as I know, no comparable work which covers so much ground so readably. It does more than fill a void.

MARTIN MEARS (President of the Law Society 1995/1996)

22nd March 1999

Acknowledgments

First, I thank Mark Lewis, Michael Moss and David Wyld, each of whom has a wealth of experience as a practising solicitor, for their constructive criticism and Jonathan Pearce of Legal Action Group for his helpful suggestions. I am grateful to the Law Society's Research and Policy Unit for their statistics and Neil Casson of the Solicitors' Indemnity Fund for his assistance with the Solicitors' Indemnity Rules 1997. I am also grateful to Peter Ross, Director of the Office for the Supervision of Solicitors, for his encouragement in the writing of this book.

I wish to thank my wife, who read and approved the text from a layman's point of view.

I am particularly grateful to Martin Mears, Past President of the Law Society, for his foreword, although it should be understood that any textual errors are entirely my responsibility.

I would especially thank Angela Buckenham for her careful typing of my original work, the many revisions and the final script.

L. K.

Preface

The purpose of this book is threefold: first, to provide the general public with a brief outline of the role of the solicitors' profession and to summarize how a person qualifies to become a solicitor and how he is regulated; secondly, to inform clients what they are entitled to expect from their solicitor; and thirdly, to set out the client's rights and remedies against his solicitor.

Although this book contains no new material, it does for the very first time set out these matters in what is hoped to be a logical order from the client's as well as the solicitor's point of view.

It is divided into three compact parts titled "Part I - The Solicitor," "Part II - You with Your Solicitor" and "Part III - You against Your Solicitor."

The text includes references to the principles extracted from the Guide to the Professional Conduct of Solicitors 1996 Seventh Edition e.g. "12.06" is a reference to Principle 12.06 "A Solicitor must carry out a client's instructions diligently and promptly".

Where appropriate, the text refers to relevant sections of the Solicitors Act 1974; for example, "s1(a)" is a reference to paragraph (a) of section 1 of the Solicitors Act 1974. The precise wording of the sections or parts of sections referred to is set out in Appendix 1.

In addition to them being explained and summarised in the text, the Solicitors' Accounts Rules 1991 are set out virtually verbatim in Appendix 2. The relevant rules of court are contained in Appendix 3; there is also a precedent for a claim for professional negligence in Appendix 4.

Laurence Kingsley.

PART I : THE SOLICITOR

Introduction

In the beginning - after he had created the heaven and the earth, light and darkness, the land and the sea and all the creatures of the earth - God created Adam. "And God saw everything that he had made, and behold, it was very good. And it was evening and it was morning, the sixth day."

But then, God planted a garden in Eden and placed Adam within it; God saw that it was not so good for Adam to be alone; and from his rib he created and gave woman to man; and it was still good but not quite so good. It gets worse!

The world of Adam and Eve was extremely permissive; only to eat of the fruit in the midst of the garden was forbidden to them. Enter the serpent - the first lawyer - to question the validity of this prohibition. Easily persuaded by the silver tongued serpent, Eve eats of the forbidden fruit and gives it to Adam to eat and their eyes were opened. Thus did God create the real world: Adam and Eve, their knowledge and their lawyer!

*   *   *   *

As at 31 July 1998 there were 95,521 solicitors (an increase of more than 4% over the previous year),of whom 75,072 (a 4.8% increase) held practising certificates. Of these, 4,661 were working in commerce or industry, 2,845 in local government,1,525 with the Crown Prosecution Service, 2,053 in sundry occupations such as accountants firms, nationalised industries, trades unions, government departments, court clerks, government-funded services, citizens advice bureaux, education establishments, the National Health Service, the armed forces and religious institutions and a further 3,170 not categorised and possibly unemployed. There were therefore 60,818 solicitors in private practice with 9,743 firms. As for the firms themselves 4,676 were sole practitioners, 3,627 were firms with two to four partners, 1,002 firms with five to ten partners, 314 firms with 11 to 25 partners and 124 with 26 or more partners. Almost all categories increase each year.

The mere mention of a solicitor can provoke conflicting emotions in even the most balanced of people. Solicitors are often as feared and disliked by their clients as they are revered and obeyed by them. As a body, solicitors are despised, joked about and may be the least popular of all professions. Even the judges, who were in former times always ex-barristers, purport to dislike them. "As it has been flippantly expressed, they [the judges] deprive him [the solicitor] of his bread and butter, and call it striking him off the roll."

Because of the prominent part played by solicitors in the law their activities have themselves been subject to the approval of the judges. There has been some type of formal statutory control since at least 1728. The current Act of Parliament is the Solicitors Act 1974, many of the sections of which are dealt with in this book. In addition, the Council of the Law Society has made rules governing the professional practice, conduct and discipline of solicitors. It is these rules, which are to be found in "The Guide to the Professional Conduct of Solicitors" (7th ed, Law Society) and to which frequent reference is made in this book.

The principal watchdog of the solicitors' profession is the Law Society, which is composed entirely of solicitors and of which most solicitors are members. The Law Society exists to make rules for the profession and to enforce them through its regulatory arm, the Office for the Supervision of Solicitors. Its other main function is as a type of trade union for the solicitors' profession. It performs this task by providing spokesmen to the media to explain the role and enhance the reputation of the profession generally and by making representations to various bodies, such as the government, the Legal Aid Board, the Lord Chancellor's Department and the judiciary. Finally, the Law Society's visible and practical benefit is to be found in Chancery Lane, where it has splendid premises including restaurants, meeting rooms and a library; these facilities are of considerable benefit to solicitors and, apart from the library, their guests.

(a) Why should you have a solicitor?

There is no law that says a private individual must have a solicitor. The law and legal proceedings, however, can often be complex or uncertain. The rules of procedure are not always a matter of mere common sense and the style or format of pleadings (i.e. setting out your claim or defence to a claim) can seem strange to a layman. In addition, even a born speaker is not automatically his own best advocate. Then, of course, there are all the other difficulties, such as where to find the law, how to know what the next step is, whether you need a licence, whether an interest has to be registered somewhere - to name but a few of them.

Thus, the growth of the legal profession is easy to understand. The chances are therefore that, provided you can afford it and possibly even if you cannot afford it, you will want to employ a lawyer to take on your case, particularly where there is a lot at stake.

So, if buying a home, you will want to be sure that you have obtained legal title to your flat or house. Similarly, if you have been appointed an executor under someone's will or even, when that person dies without making a will, you are his personal representative and accordingly an administrator, it is quite likely that you will not wish to be burdened with the responsibility of dealing with the estate personally, especially as there are detailed rules to be followed and tax to be accounted for. If the estate is sufficiently valuable, it is well worth instructing a solicitor, as his scale fees will be paid out of the estate. Thus you will not have spent any of your own money, unless you are a residuary beneficiary under the will.

Even if we take a totally different area of the law, you may still want to hire a solicitor. For instance, if you have been caught for speeding, it is unlikely that you would wish to employ a solicitor, as his fee is likely to be larger than the amount by which he can reduce the fine, which the justices usually impose in accordance with their own tariff. On the other hand, in a more serious driving offence, such as dangerous driving, or speeding where you already have points on your licence and thus might be disqualified, it might well be worth your while to have a professional lawyer acting for you. The same will doubtless apply if you are being prosecuted for any serious crime or even for a minor crime, involving dishonesty, such as shop lifting or fare evasion. Even if you are pleading guilty, it is far better to have an advocate presenting any mitigation!

As for civil litigation, you may soon find that, if you are unable to settle your dispute with the other party, it becomes sufficiently complex for you to need professional help; this will also relieve some of the anxiety, which invariably accompanies such protracted activities. Your solicitor should be able to give you objective advice, including telling you that you are in the wrong, thereby saving you from embarrassment and ultimate disappointment and from wasting time and money on a case likely to be lost.

When making their will, most people prefer to have it drawn up by a solicitor. Starting a new business, where you are not intending to trade under your own name, may be eased by advice from a solicitor. Going into partnership - even with a close friend or former employee - is best safeguarded by a written partnership agreement drawn up by a solicitor, even though an oral agreement is valid, subject to proof.

Those are just some of the many reasons why you might feel that you want a solicitor!

Limited companies

A limited liability company is normally expected to appear (i.e. be represented) by a solicitor but in arbitration's or small claims in the county court and in magistrates' courts limited companies may appear by a director or any authorised representative. In practice, the rule is often relaxed for ordinary claims in the county court.

(b) The Solicitor's Qualification and Experience

In order to practise as a solicitor, a solicitor must have been "admitted" as such, have his name on the Law Society's Roll of Solicitors and have a current practising certificate: s.1 and 2.03.This also applies to solicitors employed by other solicitors: s.1A.There is statutory power to make regulations for these requirements: s.28.The education and training for those who wish to become solicitors is the responsibility of the Law Society subject to the approval of the Lord Chancellor, the Lord Chief Justice and the Master of the Rolls: s.2.

There are three routes to qualifying as a solicitor:

- the law degree route;
- the non-law degree route; and
- the non-graduate route, i.e. by qualifying through the Institute of Legal Executives (ILEX).

Continuing Education
Even when qualified and actually in practice, solicitors are obliged to keep up-to-date with developments in law and practice by satisfying the requirements for 'continuing professional development' (CPD).This is usually done by participation in authorised courses requiring attendance or examination but may include writing books or articles on law and legal research. Since 1 November 1998 all solicitors have been subject to compulsory CPD.

Solicitors Act sections referred to: 1, 1A, 2 and 28.

A STRAIGHTFORWARD GUIDE TO YOU AND YOUR SOLICITOR

(c) What only solicitors may do

A qualified solicitor with a current practising certificate is entitled to:

- conduct litigation as a solicitor: s.28 of the Courts and Legal Services Act 1990;
- appear as an advocate: s.27 (of the same act); draw or prepare for fee, gain or reward certain legal documents for legal proceedings, contracts for sale of land, conveyance or transfer of real or personal estate;
- found or oppose a grant of probate or letters of administration; or
- lodge documents for registration;
- administer oaths;
- instruct counsel.

Although there are many with greater knowledge of the law, experience in it and understanding of and feeling for it, only solicitors (as defined by s.1) may act for you by starting civil or criminal proceedings in your name or defending you in civil or criminal proceedings or appear for you in court. If an unqualified person does this, he is liable to go to prison for two years and/or be fined and he can also be guilty of contempt of court: s.20. It is also a criminal offence to pretend to be or hold oneself out to be a solicitor:s.21.

None of these solicitors' rights or privileges can prevent you from acting on your own behalf as a litigant in person. In addition, there are many quasi-judicial bodies or "courts" - from committees to important tribunals - where non-lawyers are permitted to appear, represent a party and "argue their case". Even in the courts of law themselves - civil or criminal - the litigant in person is allowed to be advised by another person, known as a "McKenzie Friend". This right - only comparatively recently recognised - has been enshrined in the law: McKenzie v McKenzie [1970] 3 All ER 1034. In that case, the Court of Appeal held that any person, whether a professional or not, may attend a trial as a friend of either party, may take notes, and may quietly make suggestions and give advice to that party. Furthermore this right has been extended to hearings in chambers, where many important rights and final decisions are made. Hearings in chambers are private, being open only to the parties and their legal advisers (including McKenzie friends) and generally take place between the issue of civil or criminal proceedings and the trial of the case.

Non-solicitors may not charge a fee for conveyancing or probate work: ss.22 and 23. There are, however, exceptions: ss.22 (2)-(4) and 23 (2)-(4) and anyone may draft your will or a power of attorney. Instructing or briefing barristers (otherwise known as "counsel") is not covered by the Solicitors Act or any other act; that barristers will accept instructions only from solicitors, accountants and patent agents is due solely to the Bar's own rules of etiquette. Not suprisingly only a solicitor can sue for his fees for acting as a solicitor: s.25, although there are many consultants, including legal advisers, whose fees are recoverable in litigation as "disbursements". An uncertificated solicitor may not recover costs: s.25.

To appear in the Crown Court or High Court, a solicitor must have a higher court's qualification for criminal proceedings, civil proceedings or both.

A practising solicitor may sell property as part of his general practice or through a separate practice just like estate agents and will continue to be subject to the Indemnity Rules, Accounts Rules, Practice Rules and Conflict of Interest Rules: 26.01.

No person shall carry on investment business unless authorised (or exempted) s.3 of the Financial Services Act 1986. Consequently your solicitor may only deal with investment for you either free of charge - in which case it would not be a business - or for remuneration provided he is authorised. His firm's stationery will usually state at the bottom: "This firm is regulated by the Law Society in the conduct of Investment Business" or "Regulated in the conduct of Investment Business by the

Law Society". Without this statement or "assurance" you should not allow your solicitor to carry out investment transactions as your agent.

Only a practising solicitor may administer an oath for an affidavit: s.81 but he should not do so where he is personally interested or acting for one of the parties: s.81(2).

Although since 1 August 1995 barristers and Fellows of The Institute of Legal Executives have also been empowered to administer oaths: s.113 (1) and (10) of the Courts and Legal Services Act 1990, this is rarely met with in practice.

Solicitors Act sections referred to: 1, 20, 21, 22, 23, 25 and 81.

(d) Accounts regulations governing solicitors

In theory, you should not need to know anything about the Solicitors Accounts Rules 1991, which exist for your protection. The mere existence of the rules, however, does not automatically safeguard your money. Although non-compliance with the rules constitutes misconduct, the solicitor may not actually do what he should do. Thus, it is useful to know the background to the rules.

The objects of the Rules are to ensure (a) the fair treatment of your money and (b) the maintenance of adequate bookkeeping and records with a view to avoiding confusion between your money and your solicitor's money: 28.02.

Your solicitor is required to keep accounts in accordance with special rules: s.32 and he has to have his accounts audited and send an accountant's report relating to clients' and controlled trust money to the Law Society annually: s.34 and 1.05.Generally, subject only to a few exceptions, your solicitor has to have his books and accounts audited by a qualified professional accountant, who is himself independent and has not been subject to disqualification by his own professional body. There are detailed rules as to what solicitors may do with money received from clients or from third parties for clients. There are the following sets of rules:-

*Solicitors' Accounts Rules 1991,
*Solicitors' Accounts (Legal Aid Temporary Provision) Rules 1992,
*Solicitors' Investment Business Rules 1995, Rules 14 and 26,
*Accountant's Report Rules 1991 and
   Solicitors' Overseas Practice Rules 1990.

The Solicitors' Accounts Rules 1991 are the most important. Their effect is summarised below and relevant rules are set out in full in Appendix 2.

Client account
The stringent rules, which exist for your protection, stipulate whether money should be paid into the solicitor's client account or his office account, and regulate the transfer of monies between the two accounts. The profession is, of course, principally concerned with the clients account and that it should be wrongfully depleted or dissipated. Therefore, the rules apply mainly to the clients account. The keeping of records in respect of the office account is of little or no interest to the law society. Once the solicitor is entitled to pay money into the office account. the Law Society ceases to be interested. The solicitor's office account may, of course, be of interest to the Inland Revenue.

Your solicitor is under a duty to keep a record of all dealings with your money, including money paid on your instructions into a foreign or building society account: 28.16.

As your solicitor is required to reconcile clients' and bank accounts every five weeks, this means in practice he must make entries contemporaneously or virtually daily. Therefore, there should be little difficulty in informing you of how much money is held on your behalf: 28.18.

*These rules will shortly be replaced. See note at the end of this section.

A client account must never be overdrawn. If it is, this is because your solicitor has deliberately or negligently used your money for his own or another client's benefit.

Without an understanding of the difference between "client's money" and other money the rules are both pointless and incomprehensible. Basically they are concerned with your solicitor's obligation in respect of your money or "client's money", how it becomes client's money, when and how it ceases to be client's money and when, through his entitlement, your solicitor may use that money for paying other people (not other clients) or "paying himself.". This last he does by transferring the money from the "client's account" into his own account, which is known as an "office account".

Your solicitor must pay client's money into his client's account without delay, i.e. the same or the next working day.

Cheques/drafts
A cheque or draft sent to your solicitor to be held to the sender's order (i.e. not to be utilised without further instructions) must not be presented for payment without the sender's consent; money telegraphically transferred but to be held to the sender's order must be held in your solicitor's client account. In either case, he is obliged to return the cheque, draft or money on demand.

Money paid on account
Money paid to your solicitor generally on account of costs and disbursements must be paid into a client account until he renders his bill, whereupon he may transfer the relevant amount to the office account, or until he pays a disbursement, which he does by drawing a cheque on the client account: 28.15. Thus money paid to you by your solicitor or money received by him for payment of a disbursement must always go into the client account. If however, he has already paid your disbursement out of his own money (i.e. from the office account) when he receives money in

respect of the disbursement, he may reimburse himself by paying it straight into the office account and not the client account. If paid into the client account, he should transfer it to his office account as soon as possible, thus achieving the separation of client's and solicitor's money as precisely as possible. Where one sum of money comprising both client's and solicitor's money is received, as it can only physically be paid into one account, it may be paid into either account, provided the relevant transfer is made as soon as possible. A transfer can be made by the drawing of a cheque on either account but is more usually made by an instruction to the solicitor's bank to transfer a particular sum from one account to the other: 28.11.

If he has no money on account and renders you a bill and you pay his bill, he must pay that money into his office account. Similarly, if, say his bill is for £1,000 and he has transferred from his client's account to his office account the £500 you originally paid him on account, the balance too must go straight into his office account: 28.14.

Exceptions to using the client account
The main instances when your solicitor need not pay money into a client account are when cash is received and is to be paid direct to you or someone on your behalf or where you have instructed him to pay it into another account: 28.15. Where it is owed to your solicitor, whether it is on account of his bill or on account of an agreed fee, even though the work has not yet been completed, it must be paid into his own account: 28.15.

Interest on client accounts
By Rule 20 of the Solicitors' Accounts Rules, your solicitor must account to you for interest. This includes not only money held generally on account of costs but all money received from or for your benefit, including money for the payment of disbursements: 28.23. As your solicitor's client's account usually bears interest, it may not be used as a mere convenience by the solicitor. He must not allow the interest earned to accumulate but must transfer it to the office account or pay it to you, if you are entitled to it.: 28.12 note 2.

Non-client money

Exceptionally certain non-client money may be paid into a client's account: the main categories are trust money, money to replace a sum which has been wrongfully or inadvertently withdrawn from the client account, money comprising both client's and non-client money (see above) and money, the purpose of which is not readily apparent to the solicitor. In relation to this last category the motto seems to be "If in doubt, pay it into the client account!" and then as soon as practicable decide on its fate and direction. For example, your solicitor may have been paid by you in respect of both money on account of unbilled or future work and a disbursement, e.g. barrister's fees, and not know whether or not his accounts department has already paid counsel: 28.12.

Fraud and/or bankruptcy

As from 31 August 1998, your solicitor's accountant, in accordance with Rule 3(4) of the Accountant's Report Rules 1991 is instructed and encouraged to report directly to the Law Society without reference to your solicitor should he discover evidence of theft or fraud affecting client's money. Your solicitor must include in his accountant's retainer an instruction to report him, i.e. the solicitor, directly to the Law Society should his appointment be terminated because he is about to issue or has issued a qualified accountant's report.

If your solicitor is made bankrupt, his practising certificate is automatically suspended: s.15(1), although he maybe able to obtain reinstatement from the Adjudication and Appeals Committee of the Office for the Supervision of Solicitors (OSS): 30.05.

The Main Accounts rules

The following is a condensed or simplified version of the main or relevant rules, which should enable you (a) to understand the main objectives of the safeguards imposed on your solicitor for your benefit and (b) to know the destination of money held by him.

PART ONE THE SOLICITOR

Rule 2: defines "client's money" as being money held or received by a solicitor on account of a person for whom he is acting in relation to the holding or receipt of such money either as a solicitor or, in connection with his practice as a solicitor, as agent, bailee, stakeholder or in any other capacity; provided that the expression "client's money" shall not include -

(a) money held or received on account of the trustees of the trust of which the solicitor is a controlled trustee; or

(b) money to which the only person entitled is the solicitor himself or, in the case of a firm of solicitors, one or more partners in the firm".

Rule 3: Your solicitor should without delay pay all client's money into his client account. He may keep more than one client account.

Rule 4: Your solicitor may pay into his client account trust money, money, which may be "split" but which has not been split, and money to reimburse the account, where he has contravened the Accounts Rules. Thus it is recognised that mistakes can be made.

Rule 5A: As an exception to Rule 9(2) your solicitor may pay money in full or part settlement of a bill of costs into his client account provided that he transfers it within seven days to his office account.

Rule 6: If he pays money into his client account other than in accordance with the previous rules referred to above, he must withdraw it without delay on discovery. This again recognises that mistakes can be made.

Rule 7: Your solicitor may withdraw from his client account -

(a) in the case of your money -

(i) money payable to you or on your behalf e.g. for disbursements to third parties.

(ii) money to reimburse him for disbursements paid by him on your behalf from his office (own) account.

(iii) money drawn with your authority.

(iv) money for or towards payment of his costs where he has delivered a bill of costs or other written intimation of the amount of costs incurred and

(v) money by way of transfer to another client account.

(b) in the case of trust money -

(i) money for payment in the execution of the trust and

(ii) money to be transferred to a separate bank or building society account for or in the name of the trust.

(c) money paid into the account in contravention of Rule 6.

Rule 9: (1) Your solicitor need not pay into the client account (a) cash payable to you or on your behalf to a third party, (b) cheques or drafts, which may be endorsed by him to you or a third party or, (c) money destined for some other account chosen by you.

(2) Your solicitor must not pay into a client account money held or received by him -

(a) which you asked him in writing for your own convenience to withhold from such an account or

(b) which is to reimburse him or

(c) which is for or towards payment of his bill of costs or in respect of an agreed fee.

PART ONE THE SOLICITOR

Rule 11: (1) Your solicitor must keep properly written up accounts as may be necessary -
- (a) to show his dealings with
  - (i) your money and
  - (ii) any other money dealt with by him through a client account and
- (b) to enable him
  - (i) to show separately the amounts and types of money held in respect of each client
  - (ii) to distinguish all money... and
- (c) to show your current balance.

Your solicitor must every five weeks compare the total balances on his client account with the money held at the bank in his client account and reconcile and explain any differences.

Your solicitor must (a) for at least six years from the date of the last entry in it preserve your account and his books, ledgers and records and bank statements as printed and issued and (b) for at least two years retain himself or at his bank all cheques and other authorities for payment.

For Part II - Controlled Trusts (see Appendix 2)

For Part III - Interest (see Part II (m) and Appendix 2)
Solicitors Act Sections referred to: 15, 32 and 34. [The relevant Solicitors Accounts Rules 1991 are set out in full in Appendix 2.]

New rules
The new Solicitors' Accounts Rules 1998 dated 22 July 1998 replace the

Solicitors' Accounts Rules 1991, the Solicitors' Accounts (Legal Aid Temporary Provision) Rule 1992 and the Accountant's Report Rules 1991. The new rules commence from 30 April 2000 but may be voluntarily adopted (in their entirety, though not selectively) beforehand.

They comprise some 50 rules with five appendices, of which only rules 1 to 28 and 30 directly affect the client; the remainder relate to the regulation, monitoring and investigation of solicitors by the Law Society and to accountant's reports.

Rule 1 Principles - adds nothing new but states that a solicitor must comply with Practice Rule 1 by keeping other people's money separate from his own in a bank or building society account identified as a client account. He must only use clients' money for their own matters. He must keep proper accounts, ensure compliance with the rules and show accurately the position of each client's money, account for interest, co-operate with the Law Society and deliver the requisite annual accountant's reports.

Apart from this the changes are minimal: Rule 2 Interpretation - includes additional definitions; Rule 9 subjects to the rules solicitors, who are also liquidators, trustees in bankruptcy, Court of Protection receivers or trustees of occupational pension schemes; and Rule 22 permits a client's account to be overdrawn in certain circumstances but this exception is more apparent than real.

(e) Professional Indemnity Insurance and the Compensation Fund

Insurance
As every solicitor in private practice is required to be indemnified (i.e. insured) by the Solicitors' Indemnity Fund (SIF): s.37, your solicitor or former solicitor (even if retired), his employees and "recognised bodies

and "former recognised bodies" are insured against "loss arising from claims in respect of civil liability incurred in private practice in their aforesaid capacities or former capacities" subject to the conditions set out in Part II of the Solicitor's Indemnity Rules 1997, Rule 9: 29.01.

The solicitor does not, however, have to provide information or make contributions to the fund if he has acted for personal friends, relatives, a company wholly owned by his family or registered charities without remuneration provided that the client is notified of the lack of indemnity position in writing; nor in respect of administering oaths or affidavits: Rule 32 and 29.01 note 2. Otherwise he must have carried out the work as part of an existing practice or have set up a new practice and made contributions or have obtained a waiver of his obligations from the Society: 29.01 note 3.

The indemnity rules do not apply to solicitors or practices outside England and Wales: 29.01 note 4, which are governed by the Solicitors' Overseas Practice Rules 1990.

The indemnity limit is up to £1,000,000 for each claim: 29.01 note 11.
There are currently no plans to increase it but it may be voluntarily topped up. The cover is extremely wide, including negligence, defamation, breach of undertaking and loss from damage to or destruction of documents: 29.01 note 8 and it includes trainee solicitors, consultants, associates, foreign lawyers who are consultants, locums and their personal representatives but it is limited to those in private practice: 29.01 note 9.

Although your solicitor must be insured, he may, provided you so agree, be able to limit his liability to £1,000,000: 12.09 and to exclude his liability to third persons: 12.09 note 6.

If you or a third party make a claim against your solicitor which is likely to exceed £500 or notify an intention to do so, he must notify the fund (if the claim is covered by the fund): 29.07. Although not obliged to do so, he should notify SIF of circumstances that could give rise to a claim so that SIF may consider possible remedial action: 29.07 note 1.

As is the case in most types of insurance, your solicitor must not admit liability and, if he does so, he may be required to reimburse the SIF, should he have been prejudiced by the admission: 29.07 note 5.

If you make a claim against your solicitor or notify him of your intention to do so or if he discovers an actual omission which would justify such a claim, he is obliged to advise you to seek independent advice: 29.08.

If you refuse to seek independent advice, he should not continue to act for you unless satisfied that there is no conflict of interest: 29.08 note 2 and 15.04.

The Solicitors' Indemnity Rules 1997 are made pursuant to s.37 and Section 9 of the Administration of Justice Act 1985 by the Council of Law Society with the concurrence of the Master of the Rolls. The fund is managed and administered by Solicitors' Indemnity Fund Ltd, a company set up by the Law Society: Rule 8.

Rule 12 contains the "Definitions". The important definitions are those defining a "member": Rule 12.9 and "private practice": Rule 12.15.

Rule 14 deals with exclusions from cover, one of which Rule 14.1(f) is in respect of fraud or dishonesty. The effect of this exclusion is, in the event of the fraud or dishonesty of a sole practitioner (as opposed to his "employee"), effectively to deprive his client of cover.

On the other hand, an innocent partner may claim, if liable to his client by virtue of the fraud or dishonesty of his partner.

Compensation

The Law Society, however, also maintains the Solicitors' Compensation Fund, which is again administered by the Office for the Supervision of Solicitors (OSS): 30.07 and which covers loss arising from fraud or dishonesty.

Thus where there is fraud or dishonesty by a sole practitioner or where all partners are party to the fraud or dishonesty, such matters are for consideration by the compensation fund: see 30.07.

The principal purpose of the Fund is to compensate those who have suffered loss by reason of the dishonesty of a solicitor or his employee (see above): see also s.36 (2) - (3). The Fund is discretionary and there is a compensation fund subcommittee of the Adjudication and Appeals Committee: 30.07 note 3. The Fund is not of course for purely personal or trading debts but does include loans, if made to a solicitor in his capacity as solicitor, which are not repaid, and losses arising from failure to honour undertakings in the usual course of practice.

The Fund is a last resort, where the loss is not covered by insurance or cannot be made good by your solicitor or a third party: 30.07 note 4. It can exceptionally be used to compensate for breach of an undertaking given with a dishonest intent by a solicitor during the course of his practice: 30.07 note 6. Grants are generally limited to £1,000,000 including legal costs and interest: 30.07 note 9.

If you are dissatisfied with the OSS's handling of your claim, you may appeal to the Legal Services Ombudsman, who is appointed by the Lord Chancellor under section 21 of the Courts and Legal Services Act 1990: 30.08. and in certain circumstances may apply to the High Court for a Judicial Review of the decision of the OSS or the Ombudsman.

Solicitors Act sections referred to: 36 and 37.

(f) Conveyancing and mortgages.

Whereas most sellers accept without question, albeit reluctantly, the apparently large sums of commission payable to their estate agent, they often hope to save on conveyancing fees and may even feel that they and the other party to the transaction can use the same solicitor to achieve the common goal of transfer of property from seller to buyer. This hope or desire survives, even though, ever since solicitors abandoned scale charges, their rates are very competitive and they frequently wage a cut price war with their competitors. Unfortunately it will be rare that all parties can use the same solicitor. There is a special rule of practice covering conveyancing: Practice Rule 6 (avoiding conflicts of interest in conveyancing) and 25.

If you are buying, selling or leasing properties "for value at arm's length", i.e. with a stranger, you and the other party to the transaction cannot save costs on conveyancing by using one solicitor: 25.01(1). There are, however, exceptions:
- where both clients are established clients of the solicitor or the consideration on a sale is £10,000 or less; or
- where there is no other solicitor or licensed conveyancer reasonably available in the vicinity; or
- where the work for each of you is effectively separated in different (associated) practices and:
- neither of you was recommended or referred by the other solicitor's associated practice; and
- the transactions are separately supervised; and
- there is no conflict of interest; and
- the sale has not been negotiated by the solicitor; and
- neither party is a builder or developer of the property; and
- both parties give their written consent: 25.01(2).

Subject always to there being no conflict of interest existing or arising a solicitor may act -

(a) in an "institutional mortgage" (e.g. building society or bank loan) for both the mortgagee (lender) and the mortgagor (borrower) if he or a member of his immediate family is the mortgagor: 25.01(3) and

(b) in a private mortgage for both lender and borrower provided the transaction is not "at arm's length" i.e. it is a "friendly" rather than purely commercial transaction: 25.01(4) and

(c) in the case of an institutional mortgage for seller, buyer and lender: 25.01(5) subject to the exceptions in 25.01(2) being satisfied (see above).

It is of course a well established exception to the conflict of interest rule that your solicitor may act for you as the buyer of a property as well as for your lender, the mortgagee. As a result of the recession, there have been many claims made by building societies against solicitors for professional negligence by the solicitor in not fulfilling the terms of his retainer with the building society. This may occur where the borrower has defaulted and the building society, having repossessed, has sold for the best price but still suffered a loss. Even more unfortunately, this remains the liability of the erstwhile borrower and home owner.

Although you do not have to employ a solicitor before (selling or) buying a property, you may encounter some minor difficulty or delay because the solicitor acting for your prospective seller, who by custom has the prerogative of drafting the contract for sale, has a duty not to submit the contract for your signature before you have had a proper opportunity to obtain legal advice: 25.04. The solution is, of course, to write to him, informing him either that you will sign it when you have taken legal advice or that you acknowledge the opportunity for doing so.

If you are selling your property through a solicitor and wish to deal simultaneously with more than one prospective buyer, you must consent to your solicitor informing each prospective buyer in writing of the situation and, unless you do so, he must not continue to act for you: 25.05(2). This must be done before the submission of the contracts of sale. (Obviously it does not mean that your estate agent cannot send particulars of your property to more than one person at a time.) It does, however, affect sales of different interests in the same land, e.g. if you are selling both the freehold and the leasehold to different parties. Quite clearly a solicitor cannot act for more than one prospective buyer without there being a conflict of interest. Nor can the solicitor act for both seller and one of the prospective buyers, even where the transaction would otherwise fall within the main exception permitted by rule 6(2): see 25.01(2).

Auctions
The rule (against acting for a seller where there is more than one prospective buyer) obviously does not relate to sales by auction where all the bidders are potential buyers. In an auction, "exchange of contracts" is effected by the acceptance of the highest bid. Consequently wise bidders will have carried out their searches, considered the replies to preliminary enquiries before contract and decided that the terms of the contract are acceptable before attending the auction and putting in a bid.

Assistance with obtaining a mortgage
You will usually have investigated the obtaining of a loan from a building society or bank before you even approach your solicitor. If, however, he offers to help you, he should not send you to a tied agent but to a proper independent mortgage or insurance broker.

Completion and payment of the solicitor's bill
Unless your solicitor has at the outset made it clear that he requires to be paid his costs before completion, he cannot refuse to complete simply because you have not paid him: 25.17 and see also 14.01 but this does not apply, if for example, you have failed to put him in funds for paying a disbursement, e.g. stamp duty, without the payment of which you, the buyer, will not be able to have your title registered.

(g) How should you select your Solicitor?

Where a solicitor has been used before

If you have used a solicitor before and were happy with the service, then you should simply ask him if he can handle your latest problem. Do not assume that because he was very efficient with the drafting of your will or helping you to buy your house that he will be able competently to sue someone for you or defend you against a criminal charge. There are very few "general practitioners" and most solicitors tend to specialise.

Obviously the first question you should ask your existing solicitor is whether he would be willing to act for you with your new problem. This is best done by telephone. His immediate reaction will probably be enough to indicate if your problem is within his area of practice. It may well be that he cannot do so but that his partner can. If so, it is highly desirable that you meet that partner and satisfy yourself that you can get on with him and, more importantly, that he appears to be competent.

Unless you yourself have legal knowledge, it will be difficult to establish the depth of his legal knowledge or his competence. It will, however, soon emerge. Solicitors should be honest in respect of their expertise, if only because they would wish to avoid an action for professional negligence. Some solicitors, however, may be driven more by the prospect of fees than by honesty in their expertise.

Assuming that this is not the case, the solicitor should tell you quite frankly whether he or another member of the firm can handle the matter. If there is no-one in the firm who can, he may well recommend another firm. If this happens, you will have to restart the whole process, i.e. meet that solicitor or firm and satisfy yourself that there can be a good relationship and a competent and economic service. In all cases, do not forget to ask how much you are going to be charged or, alternatively, his or the firm's hourly rates of charging. Note also that the minimum unit of time is generally six minutes (even for a simple confirmatory telephone call).

Recommendations and other methods
If the above fails, you may be able to obtain a recommendation from a friend. In default of a recommendation, you may happen to belong to a professional organisation, trade association or trade union. These bodies may maintain lists of suitable solicitors. Other methods are:

(a) using the Yellow Pages, some similar business directory or specialist legal directory;

(b) surfing the Internet;

(c) telephoning the Law Society on 0171 242 1222 to see if they can recommend a firm - in certain areas of law the Law Society maintains specialist panels of solicitors' firms;

(d) contacting the local Citizens Advice Bureau; or

(e) walking down the high street and spotting a local firm.

If you are visiting a new firm, consider whether your reception was friendly, whether the office seemed to be presentable and efficient and possibly even the amount of papers and files lying around in your prospective solicitor's own office. None of these constitutes a vital consideration but all these small factors may help you come to a decision. Make a list of questions, note the replies and look out for any evasive answers.

Using a leading firm does not guarantee a good service. The other party or your opponent, who is also likely to be represented by a solicitor, will not be impressed by the name of the firm but only by what it actually says and does. Remember: the work that is done for you will only be as good as the person who actually does it.

PART ONE THE SOLICITOR

Deciding upon a solicitor
However you have chosen your solicitor, remember always to go through the following drill:

1. Can he do the job?
2. Has he time to do the necessary work?
3. Will he provide an efficient service?
4. Do you believe you can get on with him?
5. Who will actually be doing the work?
6. Can you afford him?

Finally, do not forget the golden rule which is: will the solicitor be dealing with the matter personally or delegating it to an assistant, a trainee solicitor, a legal executive or even a secretary?

You should not be charged for a preliminary interview, unless of course substantial time is taken up with obtaining necessary or relevant instructions.

PART II: YOU WITH YOUR SOLICITOR

(a) The Retainer or employing a Solicitor

"Retainer" simply means the written or oral agreement to provide legal advice and services. It commences the moment the agreement has been made and before any work has been carried out or payment made and lasts until it is terminated by you or your solicitor. The consequences of termination will be dealt with later in this part of the book.

If a solicitor agrees to apply for legal aid for you, this is a separate agreement, for which, unless the contrary is agreed, he is entitled to be paid. The work in respect of the application for legal aid itself may, however, be done under a "Green Form", which is a type of legal aid and does not require prior authorisation from the Legal Aid Board. If you accept an offer of legal aid, it is implied that the solicitor you are currently dealing with will be the solicitor doing the work under your legal aid certificate. Although you will both be under obligations towards each other similar to those in "private" work, the retainer will technically be between the solicitor and the Legal Aid Board, to whom both of you will be under additional obligations. Your obligations will have been brought to your attention in the offer of legal aid. The other main difference is that the solicitor is not entitled to be paid by the Legal Aid Board for any work carried out before the date of the grant of legal aid.

Can a solicitor refuse to act for you?
Unlike a barrister, a solicitor is not obliged to accept your instructions, although he must not refuse to act for you because of any prejudice and would only normally refuse to act for you where there might be a conflict of interest between you and another client or where he might be

professionally embarrassed. This could occur where, for instance, he has previously acted against you or is related to one of the parties or persons involved. Should he not wish to act for you against another solicitor because he or his partner is friendly with the other solicitor, he should help you to obtain a suitable solicitor.

When should a solicitor not act for you?
A solicitor should not act for you if he believes you are motivated solely by malice or vindictiveness: 12.01 or where he suspects that you are under duress or the undue influence of another person, in which case he should see you alone to establish whether or not this is the case: 12.03. Nor should he act for you if he has insufficient time, experience or skill: 12.02.

Furthermore, he should not act for you if you have already retained and are still employing another solicitor. If, however, you wanted to check up on your current solicitor he can give you a "second opinion" without the first solicitor being informed: 12.05.

The solicitor's duties
The solicitor should carry out the work diligently and promptly and has implied authority to carry out all routine matters in your name so as to bind you: 12.06, although it is desirable that he consults you before taking any important step especially agreeing a settlement, however favourable it may seem to him.

Once retained, the solicitor must not terminate the retainer except for good reason and on reasonable notice. Simply disagreeing on your prospect of success would probably not be a good reason, unless he felt that you had ceased to have confidence in him. Failure to provide clear instructions or make reasonable payments on account, where not excluded by the terms of the retainer, would be good reason; so too would your or his bankruptcy or mental incapacity or your involvement in money laundering: 12.10.

Where the solicitor has started the proceedings or served the defence for you, he will be "on the record" with the court and, if he wishes to cease acting for you, he must apply to come off the record, for which purpose he would have to show just cause. If you have been legally aided and had your certificate discharged or revoked, your solicitor's removal from the record is achieved by him sending a copy of the notice (of discharge or revocation) to the other parties and the court.

(b) The Fees

General
When deciding to employ a solicitor it is vitally important that, wherever possible, you agree at the outset how much his services will cost. Agreeing a fee will, to some extent, depend on the method of payment or, more precisely, who is paying. Solicitors' fees can be paid in the following ways:

- privately (i.e., by you the client out of your own pocket);
- by legal aid;
- by legal expenses insurance: 13.06;
- by using a conditional fee agreement.

For the last three methods, see later.

If the solicitor's bill cannot be accurately estimated at the outset, then you can stipulate that you do not wish to spend more than a particular sum and/or wish to be kept informed as to the costs incurred or be sent interim bills at regular intervals. Where the bill is not fixed from the outset, then it is important that the solicitor informs you of the basis for charging.

Some solicitors have an hourly rate and a rate for letters written and letters received, to which they add a "mark up", invariably 50%, whereas others quote an overall charging rate, which includes their profit: 13.06.

Even if you are not informed of an hourly rate, your solicitor is still entitled to reasonable remuneration for his services.

It is unlikely that a firm estimate can be given let alone an overall fee be agreed for litigation simply because it is virtually impossible to predict which interlocutory steps may have to be taken or the number of applications that may have to be made or resisted.

It is quite normal at the outset for your solicitor to ask for some money on account but he should not seek a disproportionate sum on account of costs for work to be undertaken: 12.07. The sum requested must be reasonable, taking into account the amount of work contemplated in the immediate future rather than your financial circumstances.

Any money paid by you to your solicitor remains yours and must be paid by the solicitor into the client account, unless it is to defray or satisfy a bill rendered to you or where you have agreed a fee: 13.07, in either of which cases it immediately becomes his money and should be paid into the office account.

Any failure to comply with the above rules may well constitute misconduct or entitle you to complain to the OSS that you have received "inadequate professional services", which might result in a reduction of your solicitor's bill.

Your solicitor should always inform you that you are primarily liable for his fees (conventionally called costs) and that even if you win your case, you may either not obtain an order for costs or, if the other party is legally aided, be unable to enforce any order for costs: 13.09. Your solicitor ought to warn you that, even if you are successful in winning your case and obtaining an enforceable order for payment of your costs by your opponent, such costs may be less than he, your solicitor, is entitled to charge you.

Determining the fee will depend on what type of legal work you have. For the purposes of fees, the Solicitors Act 1974 divides cases into:
- non-contentious business; and
- contentious business.

These terms are defined by s.87 (1).

Contentious and non-contentious business distinguished
"Contentious business" means work done by your solicitor either "as solicitor or advocate, in or for the purposes of proceedings begun before a court or before an arbitrator appointed under the Arbitration Act ..." Thus all work to do with crime or civil litigation (such as, suing someone or defending a claim) will be "contentious". Anything else, like conveyancing (e.g., buying or selling a house or flat), probate work or drafting a will, will be "non-contentious". Giving you an opinion on a matter, which is not anticipated to (but may) result in litigation, is usually "non-contentious". Work done prior to issuing contemplated proceedings, however, is "contentious".

Once a fee has been agreed, your solicitor is bound by it even though it proves to be unremunerative for him. The corollary is that, if you have signed a "non-contentious business agreement": s.57 (3) or a "contentious business agreement": s.59 (1), you will be bound, even if he has earned his fee with ease. A contentious business agreement may be made on behalf of someone else, in which case it should be approved by the taxing officer of the court before being paid: s.62. Apart from such agreements, your solicitor is not obliged to confirm fee arrangements in writing except when selling a property as opposed to merely acting for you in conveying it: 26.08.

Non-contentious business agreements
As the name "Non-Contentious Business Agreement" implies, this is quite simply a contract for services, the price, remuneration or consideration for which may be fixed or according to an hourly rate, a percentage or even a salary with or without provision for disbursements, and, provided that you

or your agent has signed it: s.57 (3), may be sued upon apparently without you having been notified of your right to remuneration and detailed assessment of costs and without the requisite one month's delay. You still, however, have the right to have the agreement taxed whereupon the court may set it aside, reduce the amount payable or make other directions: s.57 (5). Even if you do not allege that it is unfair or unreasonable, the taxing officer may additionally, if the costs were based on hourly rates for work: s.57 (6), enquire into the number of hours worked and whether they were excessive: s.57 (7).

The agreement may be made before, during or even after the relevant transaction: s.57 (1).

In non-contentious business your solicitor has a right to require payments on account of disbursements but not on account of his costs. He can, however, quite easily stipulate at the outset that it is a condition of accepting your instructions that you make a payment on account of costs. This may be helpful to the solicitor and signify a warning to you that he may well wish to charge you for such work as he may do in respect of, for example, an abortive conveyancing transaction.

Where there is no agreed condition of payment on account of costs and provided you have paid for all necessary disbursements, the solicitor cannot lawfully terminate a non-contentious retainer until the transaction has either aborted or completed, although he can always sue for his costs afterwards. You may also vary the retainer by agreeing to pay the solicitor on account of his costs simply because it would make sense not to have to go to another solicitor, who would have to start all over again.

If you mortgage property to a solicitor alone or jointly with another, the solicitor may of course charge you for negotiating the loan, checking on your title to the property, preparing the necessary documents, etc, even though the mortgage is for his benefit: s.58.

Contentious business

This distinction between contentious and non contentious business (see earlier) is important because it affects your solicitor's rights towards you not only with regard to his costs and how they may be challenged but also with regard to his right to terminate the retainer. As stated above, your solicitor may legitimately ask you for money on account as a condition of his acting for you before he starts to do any work. Any payment on account of costs should be safe - even if you change your mind - as he must place any money paid on account into a client account. It remains your money. It is not the solicitor's money until it is transferred into the office account and the solicitor must not transfer it into the office account until he has sent you a bill. However, the money in "your" (as distinct from another client's) client account can be used for legitimate disbursements: s.67."Disbursements" would be any payments made by the solicitor on your behalf to third parties with your express or implied authority. Simple examples would be paying fees to counsel, enquiry agents or experts for their reports or affidavit fees (litigation) or local authority search fees, land registry fees and stamp duty (conveyancing).

A "Contentious Business Agreement" would appear to be similar to a non-contentious business agreement save that, although it must be in writing, it apparently need not be signed by both parties; it may be relied upon by your solicitor, even if only signed by you; nor is there any statutory requirement for it to be signed by you similarly to that in s.57 (3).

Although a solicitor may limit the extent of his liability, provided this does not fall below the minimum level of cover required by the SIF: 12.09, a term in a contentious business agreement excluding liability for negligence would be void: s.60 (5).

If you make a contentious business agreement where your solicitor's fee is not going to be based on an hourly rate, this will result in the loss of your rights to taxation or detailed assessment of the bill.

PART TWO YOU WITH YOUR SOLICITOR

In contentious business, your solicitor may request you to pay him money on account by way of security for his costs and, if you refuse or fail within a reasonable time to make the payment, he may, on giving reasonable notice, terminate the retainer: s.65.

As your solicitor is personally responsible for paying the proper costs or fees (known as "disbursements") of professional agents, e.g., barristers, legal, medical and other consultants, enquiry agents, engineers, surveyors and other experts: 20.01 or foreign lawyers 20.02, it is quite normal for him to insist on payment on account from you before carrying out any further work, even though he may not have sought any money on account of his own costs from you or billed you.

During the course of contentious work, your solicitor may ask you (if permitted by the retainer) for further money on account and will be entitled to terminate the retainer or cease doing any further work, if you do not pay him a reasonable sum as requested, within a reasonable time. Even if you fail to pay him further money on account he is not entitled to terminate the retainer at such a stage as will leave you in the lurch, e.g., just before a hearing. Any money received after sending you a bill may be paid by your solicitor into the office account. Any money paid by you on account of or in satisfaction of a prior agreed fee, which could be either for contentious or non-contentious business should normally, being the solicitor's money, be paid into the office account: 14.01.

Your solicitor should, within a reasonable time: 14.07, render his bill in sufficient detail to enable you to see what work he has done: 14.08. If he sends you a "gross sum bill" (i.e., just stating the total sum due), you should ask for details or a breakdown, which should also be sent within a reasonable time. The itemised or new bill, which could be higher than the original bill, replaces it: s.64 (2).

"In a contentious matter, a solicitor may charge interest on an unpaid bill:
    (a) if the right to charge interest has been expressly reserved in the original retainer agreement or

(b) if a client has later agreed to pay it for a contractual consideration or

(c) where the solicitor has sued the client and claimed interest under Section 35A of the Supreme Court Act 1981: 14.12.

Basically a contentious business agreement survives death, incapability or change of solicitor: s.63 but as a matter of common sense the amount you are liable to pay or recoverable by your solicitor is obviously likely to be reduced by taxation.

Solicitors Act sections referred to: 57, 58, 59, 60, 61, 62, 63, 64, 65, 67 and 87.

(c) Legal Aid, Conditional Fee Agreements and Legal Expenses Insurance

Legal Aid

Many people cannot afford to pay their solicitor's proper fees but may be eligible to receive legal aid from the state. Legal aid is available for almost all types of legal work, whether you are an accused or defendant in criminal proceedings, a plaintiff or defendant in civil proceedings or a petitioner, applicant or respondent in family proceedings. Important exceptions are, however, most tribunal work (e.g. rent tribunals and industrial tribunals), defamation claims (as opposed to defending counterclaims), undefended divorces (though not ancillary proceedings), judgment summonses and arbitration's, including small claims: section 14 of the Legal Aid Act 1988 and Part II of Schedule 2. Ancillary proceedings are the really important parts of family law because they deal with maintenance, property and the rights to have the daily care of the children and see them or have them stay with you.

You should, however, note that in this context "defamation" is confined to libel and slander; thus legal aid is obtainable for malicious or injurious falsehood, slander of title and/or trade libel.

Unless your solicitor knows that you would not qualify on financial grounds, he has a duty to inform you that you may be entitled to legal aid, even though he is not compelled himself to act for legally aided clients.

Your solicitor's failure to advise you of the availability of legal aid under the Legal Aid Act 1988, where you might be entitled to financial assistance, could amount to unbefitting conduct and negligence for breach of duty owed. The duty applies throughout the retainer so that, if, having instructed your solicitor privately, your financial circumstances deteriorate, you should so inform him. If you become legally aided, the solicitor must still perform the work for you according to the same standard of care.

If you are legally aided, your solicitor has a duty to explain the effect of the statutory charge: 13.10 and you are entitled to know the level of your solicitor's charges, if you are making a contribution towards your own legal aid. The statutory charge occurs where any type of property is recovered or preserved as a result of work carried out under a legal aid certificate. The effect is that unless the legally aided person's costs are paid by, say the other party, his costs, which are paid to his solicitors, are deducted from the property including money, recovered or preserved. The deduction will be made by the solicitor or the Legal Aid Board.

Conditional fee agreements
A conditional fee agreement is a method of funding a case on a private or non-statutory basis. The advantages are that you will not have to fund your own litigation. You will pay nothing on account and should not have to pay the solicitor at all. If the case is won, the solicitor should be able to collect the costs from the other party. The disadvantages are: first, unlike legal aid, you will be liable, if you lose, to pay the other, successful, party's costs, although this can sometimes be avoided by legal expenses insurance; secondly, because of the risk that the solicitor is taking by funding the whole process, the solicitor is entitled to increase his legal costs to well above what would normally be recoverable; and thirdly, also by virtue of the potential risk to the solicitor, the solicitor is unlikely to

take on the case on a conditional fee basis at all, unless he believes that the prospect of success is as near to certain as possible.

Conditional fee agreements, introduced by s.58 of the Courts and Legal Services Act 1990, came into force on 5 July 1995 and permitted solicitors to enter into "no win, no fee" agreements for personal injury, insolvency and European Commission of Human Rights and European Court of Human Rights cases with non-legally aided clients: 14.06. As the government intends to extend the scope of conditional fee agreements, thereby reducing the need for legal aid, these agreements will gradually become more and more important.

Advertisements which purport to offer a solicitor's services on the basis that the client is, for example, able to litigate "at no financial risk" would be misleading.

Do not ask your solicitor to act on a contingency (as opposed to a conditional) fee basis, as this is unlawful: 14.04.

By Rule 18 of the Solicitors' Practice Rules (2) (Interpretation) (a) an "arrangement" means any express or tacit agreement between a solicitor and another person whether contractually binding or not and (c) a "contingency fee" means any sum (whether fixed, or calculated either as a percentage of the proceeds or otherwise howsoever) payable only in the event of success in the prosecution or defence of any action, suit or other contentious proceeding. The Law Society is, however, reviewing this rule. A contingency fee does not include a pure fixed fee win or lose.

You and your solicitor may, however, agree a percentage or commission on debt collecting up until when it is necessary to start an action: 14.05 note 3.

Legal expenses insurance
Where you have been recommended to or are covered by legal expenses insurance, although your solicitor has a duty to your insurers to mitigate your loss and keep them informed of progress, his principal duty is to you:

6.01 note 1. Your right to the solicitor of your choice is subject only to the terms of your insurance policy. He is not allowed to pay a fee or commission to the introducer i.e. the person who recommended you: note 4 and he should inform you that you remain responsible for paying him, if your insurers refuse to do so: note 5. The solicitor's duty of confidentiality is subject only to your obligation to make disclosure to your insurers and he should obtain your consent before allowing them to inspect your file: 6.02. Termination of insurance cover does not affect you or your solicitor's right to terminate the retainer: 6.03.Legal expenses insurers' own employed solicitors may act in non-personal injury claims but only up to the "no costs" limit: 6.04.

As many household contents and motor insurers, including motor breakdown cover companies, provide for the payment of your own and the other side's legal costs, you should check your policies. Trade union membership usually confers similar benefits. There is also "after the event" insurance. If your solicitor is a panel member, the insurers will indemnify you against the cost of litigation, should you lose, provided they are willing to assume the risk, for which purpose they will assess your prospects and decide on the appropriate premium.

(d) What should you expect from your solicitor? What may he do and not do for you?

As the client, it is your solicitor's duty to act in your best interests subject only to his overriding duty to the court and the public interest: Solicitors' Practice Rules 1990, rule 1.

What this means in practice?
The term 'best interests' means two things:
- that your solicitor must be your advocate; and
- that your solicitor must be objective

Your advocate
Your solicitor is your advocate; he is not meant to be impartial in the

same way as a judge. He should therefore put your case, both verbally or in correspondence, pleadings or affidavits, in the best light possible and should argue it, when acting as an advocate or negotiator, as favourably as possible and as forcefully as he can. Many clients are impressed by aggressive advocates but few lawyers are cowed by them. Persuasion is therefore preferable to unreasoned passion.

Objectivity
Equally important as being your advocate, your solicitor has a duty to advise you as objectively as possible. This includes informing you of:

- the strengths and weaknesses of your case;
- the desirability of trying to settle it;
- the availability, if appropriate, of legal aid;
- the possibility of mediation (or Alternative Dispute Resolution);
   and the situation as to both the amount of costs being incurred by you to him and the potential costs being incurred by you to the other side, were you to lose or have to discontinue your case.

Possible conflicts
The solicitor's role towards you may seem obvious but has to be stated. It is, however, always subject to and may conflict with his overriding duties (see below), i.e., his duties to the court and to the public interest. These duties are virtually the same but there can be differences.

Solicitor's duty to the court
The solicitor's duty to the court is, quite simply, not to mislead it. It is impossible to give an exhaustive list in this book. An important example, however, is your (or his) affidavit in support of your application for an ex parte injunction (i.e. where the other party is not present). In this situation he must, perhaps surprisingly, bring to the court's attention any points adverse to your claim; secondly, in the absence of the other party, he should not mislead the court; and thirdly, he must not adduce evidence from you or a witness, which he knows to be false; this would be seen as

especially pertinent in criminal cases: see also Litigation and Advocacy (below).

Solicitor's duty to the public interest
An example of acting against the public interest would be any attempt, albeit indirectly, to pervert the course of justice such as by threatening a witness.

Other duties
A solicitor has also to maintain his independence, integrity and the good repute of the profession.

Independence
Maintaining independence means that the solicitor must not allow himself to be used by you as a vehicle for fraud or anything improper. It also means that he must not require that another party be represented by a particular solicitor: 1.02 note 7 or any solicitor other than X; nor may he disable himself from acting for any litigant.

Integrity
Maintaining integrity does not mean being impartial; it means that the solicitor must not allow himself to do anything improper, however assiduously he is advocating your cause.

The profession's good repute
Maintaining the profession's good repute means that he must not professionally or otherwise, whether on his own or your behalf, act fraudulently, deceitfully or contrary to his position as solicitor or take unfair advantage of another: 17.01. You should not ask or expect him to behave rudely or write offensive letters to the other party, his solicitor or, indeed any other person. This need not prevent him from driving a hard bargain.

What cases should a solicitor not take on?
Your solicitor should regard himself as being subject to the CCBE

(Counsel of the Bars and Law Societies of the European Community) Code of Conduct for Lawyers in the European Community, Article 3 of which deals with "Relations with Clients" and, in respect of paragraph titled "3.1 Instructions", states:

3.1.1 "A lawyer shall not handle a case for a party except on his instructions. He may, however, act in a case in which he has been instructed by another lawyer who himself acts for the party or where the case has been assigned to him by a competent body.

3.1.2 A lawyer shall advise and represent his client promptly, conscientiously and diligently. He shall undertake personal responsibility for the discharge of the instructions given to him. He shall keep his client informed as to the progress of the matter entrusted to him.

3.1.3 A lawyer shall not handle a matter which he knows or ought to know he is not competent to handle, without co-operating with a lawyer who is competent to handle it. A lawyer shall not accept instructions unless he can discharge those instructions promptly having regard to the pressure of other work."

Your solicitor may, however, communicate with your debtor's employer as to his status or means but must not use the threat of contacting the employer or the media as a lever to obtain payment: 17.05 note 2.

You must not expect your solicitor to seek from another party, your own legal costs, when writing a letter before action: 17.05 because such costs are not legally recoverable at that stage.

You cannot use your own or the other party's solicitor for the purpose of swearing an affidavit or making a declaration: 17.07 and s.81 (2).

Even though you have a solicitor acting for you and are already involved in litigation, your dispute can still be submitted to the comparatively new processes of mediation or Alternative Dispute Resolution.

PART TWO YOU WITH YOUR SOLICITOR

Executors and wills
If you are an executor under a will and you instruct a solicitor to handle the probate, you are the client; as a beneficiary, however, you will have no right to a copy of the file of the solicitor handling the probate, even though there are no lay personal representatives.

Children
Other instances of you being the client, where it is not immediately obvious, are those where you have instructed the solicitor on behalf of your child or a person with a disability. Theoretically your child, for whom you will be his "next friend", or the person with the disability will be the actual client but obviously for all practical purposes the instructions will have to come from you and you will be the recipient of the solicitor's advice. In these sort of cases, it can eventually transpire, where a potential conflict of interest arises, that you and, say your child, have to be separately represented or advised.

Solicitors Act sections referred to: s.81.

(e) Instructing your Solicitor; What your Solicitor should expect from you.

(i) Instructing your Solicitor
A solicitor may not act for you without your instructions to do so. In theory, he acts as your agent and therefore everything is done in your name. It follows that everything done must be with your authority. In practice, you may well only give him one express instruction at the outset of the retainer, when you ask him to buy a house for you, sue someone or defend proceedings brought against you.

What is the scope of your solicitor's authority?
Once he has express authority for a particular matter or case, he will automatically have implied authority to do everything necessary for the furtherance of the transaction or case. Your solicitor may well need information and documents. To this end, many solicitors ask their clients

to complete questionnaires, especially with regard to standard matters like conveying property, making a will, family proceedings and personal injury or road traffic accident cases. Do not take offence by regarding this as impersonal. From his point of view, it is probably more efficient and ultimately for your own good by saving you costs!

Give your solicitor all the facts and documents
In non-standard matters, such as most litigation, he is likely to ask you to draft a statement and/or ask you a series of questions on specific points. He will also expect you to provide him with all relevant documents. So that the case can be dealt with as efficiently and effectively as possible, it is best to help your solicitor by providing him at the outset with the relevant information and documents. All that you supply to the solicitor forms part of your instructions to him. The more information you supply, and the better the method of supply, then the more likely that your case will be handled well.

Following your case
Although you are entitled to know precisely what he is doing for you and why it is necessary, you cannot expect him to give you detailed explanations of all the various rules of evidence and procedure without charging you for his time. Do not therefore expect him to send you copies of every document sent and received; if you do, which you are entitled to do, he is entitled to charge you for it. There is an old saying that you should not hire a dog, if you wish to bark yourself!

Solicitors do not all work the same way
Some solicitors like to deal with one stage at a time, in which case you are likely to hear from your solicitor quite frequently; other solicitors prefer to obtain all their information, if possible, at the outset, in which case you may not hear from them for some time. Provided you have confidence in both his competence and his application, the best advice is to let him get on with it in his own way, although it is not unreasonable to expect to be kept informed of the progress of your case from time to time.

Some clients, being somewhat anxious, telephone their solicitor to tell him that they are about to send him a letter. They then send it. Shortly thereafter they telephone to check that it has been received. In such a case, should he wish to do so, your solicitor is entitled to charge you for two telephone attendances in addition to any work pursuant to the receipt of your letter. It is therefore in your own interests to avoid making unnecessary or excessive contact. There are, however, certain things that you must do personally such as swearing an affidavit or signing a will.

In litigation, you are likely to have to provide your solicitor with specific authorities for him to act. For example, you have a duty fully to disclose all relevant documents (formerly known as "making discovery"). Your solicitor may not mention this duty as such or use this terminology. He is more likely to say: "Have you given me every relevant document in the case? If not, please will you do so." When you comply with his request, you will in effect be instructing him by putting him in a position to discharge your duty as a litigant. You will also be impliedly authorising or instructing him to make use of the information and documents for this purpose.

Can you choose your own barrister?
Although the Guide to the Professional Conduct of Solicitors is strangely silent on the most important question of whether the client may select counsel, you do have the right personally to choose your own barrister. If you chose to exercise this right by nominating a barrister, whom you know or have heard of, your solicitor still has a duty to discuss and advise you on his suitability: 7.02 note 4(b). Should you not instruct your solicitor to employ a particular barrister, he will have implied authority to make a suitable choice.

By rule dated 18 January 1995 the Council of Law Society with the concurrence of the Master of the Rolls under s.31 and Section 9 Administration of Justice Act 1985 introduced the Solicitors' Anti-Discrimination Rule 1995. As from 18 July 1995 a solicitor must not discriminate on grounds of race or sex or unfairly or unreasonably on ground of disability in their professional dealings with clients, staff, other solicitors, barristers or other persons.

(ii) What your solicitor should expect from you

Your solicitor will expect only four things from you:

(i) frankness;
(ii) clear instructions;
(iii) prompt payment on account of his costs and your disbursements and the payment of his bill; and
(iv) your attendance at court, when necessary.

If, in addition, you are a grateful client, that will be a bonus.

In order that he may be paid for his services your solicitor must deliver a signed bill. When he does so, he is entitled to be paid by you or, if he holds money to your credit, to transfer from his client's account such sum as will settle his bill to you in part or in full.

Delivery of a bill as a matter of law comprises three elements. First, although the bill may be a "gross sum" bill, it should contain sufficient information to enable you to assess it or be advised as to whether or not it should be taxed (this is where the court decides on the justification for and fairness of the legal costs claimed by your solicitor: see Part III (e) below). In the absence of sufficient detail, there is no "bill" as a matter of law. Secondly, either the bill itself must be signed or it must be sent with a letter signed by him in his own or his firm's name: s.69 (2)(a). Thirdly, it must be "delivered" by being handed to you personally or sent by post or left with your agent or servant, authorised for this purpose. It cannot simply be sent to your new solicitor, unless he is your agent authorised for this purpose: s.69 (2)(b).

If the above three requirements are satisfied, then the solicitor may sue you for his unpaid costs, but not until one calendar month after delivery of

the bill. Exceptions to this one-month time limit include a belief that you are:
   (a) about to leave the jurisdiction;
   (b) about to be made bankrupt or intending to compound with your creditors; or
   (c) likely to do something tending to prevent or delay payment: s.69(1).

For the purpose of obtaining his costs by an action against you, this includes a counterclaim. He may, however, sue you on an account stated without having delivered the signed bill and also his costs may be the subject of a set off i.e., defence to an action by you. Furthermore, a statutory demand, which is a preliminary step prior to making someone bankrupt may, as it is not an action, be served by him on you before one month has elapsed.

Solicitors Act section referred to: 69.

(f) Client Care

In order to combat the increasing number of complaints against solicitors, the Law Society has sought to avoid breakdowns in the professional relationship between client and solicitor. To this end, i.e. to foster client care, it has recommended that your solicitor should, at the very outset of the relationship, tell you "how to complain" and possibly provide you with a complimentary copy of this book. The ever increasing number of complaints about solicitors has justified the profession's comparatively recent policy in having introduced a complaints procedure.

The right to complain
Since 30 April 1991 your solicitor has been under a duty by virtue of Rule 15 of the Solicitors' Practice Rules to tell you in writing how to complain, to whom in the firm and his status: 13.01. This will usually take the form of an internal complaints procedure and is often accompanied by information on how to complain to the Office for the Supervision of Solicitors. Your solicitor, however, would not have to do this, if you had

been his client since before 1 May 1991. It would also be inappropriate for him to give you this information, if you have recently been bereaved or have sought his help in an emergency.

What you should be told
Although you have gone to a solicitor because you are unable or do not wish to handle the matter yourself, it does not follow that he has to keep you informed of every little thing that happens. He should carry out the work diligently and promptly and has implied authority to carry out all routine matters in your name so as to bind you: 12.06, although it is desirable that he consults you before taking any important step, especially agreeing a settlement, however favourable it may seem to him.

It is a reasonable expectation of any professional service, however, to expect to be kept informed as to progress, delay, the receipt of important information and the taking of important decisions; certainly if you request information, explanation or advice, you are entitled to receive it. After all, that is why you retained him: 13.04. In short, your solicitor should report to you from time to time and on all important matters. Where there is a choice between alternative courses, whether in non-contentious or contentious matters, he should provide you with sufficient information and advice to enable you to make an intelligent and reasoned choice as well as giving you his own opinion.

Essential Information
If you are buying a property, he should report on title; if you are a plaintiff or defendant, he should explain the likely stages of the case, the timescale and the outcome, the possibility of Legal Aid being available and the risk of having to pay the other side's costs; if you are leasing land, he should explain the important covenants i.e. your obligations to your landlord; if he is advising you to discontinue your case, he should explain to you his reasons for not expecting you to win or thinking you will lose and not simply say that, unless you take his advice, he will not continue to act for you; if a payment into court has been made by the defendant to satisfy

your claim, he should explain why he thinks you should accept it, even though it is less than your claim, and the consequences as to costs, if you refuse to accept the offer; if you are a plaintiff, he should inform you as to the response, if any, to his "letter before action"; he should obtain your specific authority to commence proceedings; he should send you copies of important documents like draft pleadings before he serves them on the other side; he should seek your comments on the defence; he is likely to send you any request for further particulars from the other side, if only to obtain your instructions; he should inform you of any offer made by the other side, even if it is derisory; he should obtain your express authority to accept a settlement; and, if you are a defendant, he will have to report to you at appropriate stages.

After you have instructed him and at the outset, he should provide you with his opinion on the merits of your claim. He should discuss fees with you: see (b) The Fees (above).

Most importantly, according to the CCBE Code of Conduct for Lawyers in the European Community, your solicitor should not leave you in the lurch. Article 3.1.4 states:

"A lawyer shall not be entitled to exercise his right to withdraw from a case in such a way or in such circumstances that the client may be unable to find other legal assistance in time to prevent prejudice being suffered by the client." This would apply even if you were to refuse or be unable to pay him a reasonably demanded sum on account of costs.

Finally, although you may expect and receive consideration and sympathy, do not be disappointed if he wishes "to keep his distance"; he is advised not to give presents (other than the occasional cigarette or drink for immediate consumption in his presence) and it might amount to an abuse of his fiduciary relationship for him to enter into a sexual relationship with you: 12.07.

(g) Confidentiality
Can you confide in your solicitor?
So soon as you have retained your solicitor and even before he starts to act on your behalf it is very likely that he will have acquired confidential information. He is also likely to obtain information from others that will be of relevance to the matter, with which he is dealing, and of importance to you.

The duty of confidentiality is both obvious and extremely wide. In short, virtually any information - however seemingly innocuous - acquired by your solicitor during the retainer, is confidential and remains so even after the matter has been completed or the retainer terminated. An obvious example of confidentiality is your address: 16.04.

Your solicitor's duty of confidentiality is shared by his staff: 16.01. Breach of this duty is a ground for both disciplinary proceedings and an action for damages for breach of confidence. As previously stated, it continues after termination of retainer and on death passes to your personal representatives. If a solicitor obtains confidential information on your behalf, he is still bound by his duty of confidentiality even if never retained by you. Obviously if you instruct him jointly with another, information obtained from or for only one of you must be shared with the other. It may not, however, be disclosed to a third person without the consent of you both.

Your solicitor must not profit by using your confidential information for his own benefit: 16.05 and, if he does so, you may sue him for an account of profits.

Just as he has a duty to keep information imparted to him by you or others confidential so he has a duty to pass on to you any information received by him: 16.06 and, if he fails to do so, he may be liable to you for damages and will be liable to professional disciplinary proceedings. From this it follows that he should not pass on to the other party's solicitor confidential information that he does not wish to be imparted to the other party;

equally, he should not agree to accept information on condition that he does not pass it onto you. Exceptionally, he would not be liable for not telling you something potentially harmful to your own mental or physical condition such as the existence of a medical report, stating that you are suffering from a terminal illness.

If he is in possession of information acquired through discovery (i.e. disclosure of documents), the information remains confidential unless and until it has been referred to in open court. Therefore he should not act for another party, to whom that information might be useful: 1.02 note 7(b).

Exceptions to the duty of confidentiality
One exception to the rule as to confidentiality can arise quite normally where your solicitor settles your claim and the settlement includes a term that the other party should pay you your costs; then, since he must give that person an opportunity of agreeing your costs or having them assessed by the court: 17.03, this may include providing the other party with a breakdown of his costs, whether contentious or non-contentious.

Another normal exception concerns powers of attorney. In powers of attorney the donee of a power is the donor's agent; there is therefore no duty of confidentiality between the two and thus anything said by either the donee or the donor to the solicitor may be passed on to the donor or the donee respectively: 24.03.

The solicitor, who drafted a will which is being disputed, may disclose information concerning the making of the will to persons other than the personal representatives, provided there is no conflict of interest.

In the case of a joint retainer, and so soon as there arises a conflict between your solicitor's duty to disclose information to you, which is injurious to his other client or vice versa, he must cease acting for one or both of you: 15.03 (see under Conflict of Interest).

The above exceptions arise from the very nature of the transaction or case. Other "free-standing" exceptions to the duty of confidentiality must now be considered. Your solicitor is not bound by his duty of confidentiality if:

(a) you consent to disclosure;

(b) disclosure is necessary to prevent serious bodily harm;

(c) he suspects that you have committed certain criminal offences, (Your solicitor will commit a crime under Section 26B of the Drug Trafficking Offences Act 1994 and Section 18A of the Prevention of Terrorism (Temporary Provisions) Act 1989 if he does not tell the police of his suspicions of your activities. He also has a duty as to disclosure if he suspects that you are using him for money laundering purposes. Therefore be careful what you tell him! Nor is he allowed to give you a "tip off". There is, however, all the difference in the world between helping you to commit a crime and advising you as to whether a proposed course of action is legal or illegal, which is perfectly proper.)

(d) in child abuse cases;
(Where you inform your solicitor that you intend to kidnap or abduct (take without all the appropriate consents) a child or have done so, your solicitor is released from his duty of confidentiality and must disclose the information to the court. For anything less than kidnapping or abduction, however, the duty of confidentiality subsists subject to there being exceptional circumstances, such as the wider public interest, justifying disclosure.

If you tell your solicitor you are proposing to kidnap, abduct or abuse a child, he must advise you by explaining the crime of kidnapping, the offences under the Child Abduction Act 1984, the provisions of the Child Abduction and Custody Act 1985 and any other relevant crimes or offences. If this advice is sufficient to cause the wrong to cease, his duty of confidentiality is reintroduced.)

(e) with regard to certain experts' reports;

(Should your solicitor receive a psychiatrist's report, containing information that you are likely to commit a crime, like murder, grievous bodily harm or abuse on a child, he would again have to wrestle with his conscience before divulging the information to the police and the potential victim.)

(f) a court orders disclosure;

(Obviously, a solicitor's duty of confidentiality is overruled if a court orders that the information must be disclosed.)

(g) it is a matter of public record;

(Again, the duty of confidentiality is irrelevant if the information in question is readily available to the general public in some way, shape or form.)

(h) it has to be reported to the Legal Aid Board;

(If you are legally aided, your solicitor's duty of confidentiality is subject to him informing the Legal Aid Board, if you have required him to conduct your case unreasonably or so as to incur unjustifiable expense or failed to furnish requisite information or, when so doing, made a false statement or representation. He is also under a duty to inform the Legal Aid Board if you refuse to accept a reasonable settlement or payment into court: Regulation 70, Civil Legal Aid (General) Regulations 1989. Privilege and confidentiality may also be overridden by Regulation 73, if he is required to provide information about you or your case to the Legal Aid Board.)

(i) you become insolvent (i.e. bankrupt);

(Your solicitor may have to divulge confidential information, in the case of your insolvency, to your trustee in bankruptcy or, in the case of your company's insolvency, to liquidators, provisional liquidators, administrators, administrative receivers and the Official Receiver. This latter does not apply if your solicitor was acting for you, personally or as a director, as opposed to acting for the company.

It is unclear whether your trustee in bankruptcy's right overrides your solicitor's duty on privilege and confidentiality in respect of information imparted by you in order to resist bankruptcy proceedings whether before or after bankruptcy.)

(j) he requires the information to defend himself against a complaint by you to the police or the Office for the Supervision of Solicitors.

(h) Conflicts of Interest

Conflicts of interest may occur between client and client or between client and solicitor.

Inter-client conflict arises where the duty to maintain confidentiality on behalf of one client conflicts with the duty to impart information obtained to the other client.

A conflict of interest could occur at any time. There should be no excuse for a conflict existing at the outset of the retainer, although it may well happen, when a solicitor does not realise that he or another member of his firm has acted or is already acting for a client, whose interests conflict with your own.

What happens when there is a conflict?
Your solicitor should not agree to act for another person, if this is likely to result in there being a conflict of interests: 15.01. See also CCBE Article 3.2.1, which states:

"A lawyer may not advise, represent or act on behalf of two or more clients in the same matter if there is a conflict, or a significant risk of a conflict, between the interests of those clients".

This could occur where you are a client jointly with another person. At all times the emphasis is on the confidential information being relevant. If a conflict arises, your solicitor should normally cease to act for both parties: 15.03.

During the course of his acting for you, it is more than likely that he obtained confidential information about you. After ceasing to act for you, he must neither act for another person against you: 15.02 nor make use of the information without your consent. Such situations often occur, where solicitors have acted for husband and wife, who later fall out, or a family, where one of the members of the family becomes at loggerheads with the others. It can also occur where he acted for borrower and lender, partners, local authorities, who might have disputes with other clients of his, or even when he changes firms.

Ideally your solicitor should not put you in any position, where it could be said that he had benefited you by virtue of any office, appointment or position held by him e.g. local authority councillor, prosecutor, part-time judge, clerk to the justices, member of the Gaming Board, coroner, member of a police authority, legal aid committee or Criminal Injuries Compensation Authority.

A STRAIGHTFORWARD GUIDE TO YOU AND YOUR SOLICITOR

What happens with mergers of firms?
The problem of conflict of interest is increased where two or more firms amalgamate. If your solicitor's firm merges with a solicitor acting for the other party, the new firm should cease to act for both of you but it may continue to act for one of you with the other party's consent: 3.14 note 3. Equally if your solicitor's firm is taken over, the new firm should inform you and tell you the amount of your credit in the client's account and that, unless they hear from you to the contrary within a specified time, they will continue to deal with your matter: 3.14 note 5.

In non-contentious matters, the new firm may act for both you and its other client provided (a) you both consent, (b) it remains in each client's best interest for it to continue to act, (c) neither solicitor will be embarrassed, (d) neither of you may be favoured and (e) the risks have been fully explained to both of you. Although exceptionally there may be a "Chinese wall", practical difficulties are almost inevitable. A "Chinese wall" cannot be used in litigation: Annex 15A.

What is client/solicitor conflict?
Client/solicitor conflict may not always be so easy to recognise as it often arises out of what appears to be a mutually beneficial transaction. In this case, the principle would appear to be that either what is beneficial for your solicitor is not beneficial for you or the benefit conferred on the solicitor is likely to diminish his independence of mind or detract from his integrity.

Your solicitor must not act for you, where his own interest conflicts with yours: 15.04. You may, during the course of a transaction or an ongoing relationship, wish to confer a benefit on him by a loan or gift. Even though a loan between you and your solicitor or a sale or purchase of property from one to the other is intended to benefit both of you, there is inevitably a conflict of interest and your solicitor must only proceed with the transaction after he has given you the opportunity of obtaining independent legal advice.

Although he may obtain security for his costs from you or take a charge over your property, he should invite you to seek independent legal advice so as to avoid an allegation by you that he has exercised undue influence.

Independent advice is not confined to legal advice. His obligation to suggest that you obtain independent advice is not over-ridden by your having given him a power of attorney.

The same principles apply to any significant gift whether inter vivos or by will: 15.05 and extends to members of your solicitor's family or staff. This of course does not apply, where you leave property to your solicitor for the purpose of him carrying out your wishes. In such a case he should ensure that the terms of any such secret trust are contained in a separate written document, which you should sign or initial.

If your solicitor is of the opinion that your wishes as a beneficiary conflict with your duties as a personal representative, you may have to go to another solicitor to advise you on your personal position.

For conflicts in conveyancing: see Part I (f).

(i) Relationship with other solicitors

Your solicitor's overriding duty to you must always be tempered with frankness and good faith towards other solicitors: 19.01. His fraud, deceit, dishonouring of his word or undertaking may render him liable to disciplinary action or possibly even civil or criminal proceedings.

Solicitors to third parties
If another party is represented by a solicitor, your solicitor should write to that person's solicitor or ask to be put in touch with him. If he wishes to contact him direct, he should seek the other party's solicitor's consent: 19.02. If, however, the other solicitor fails to reply or pass on messages to his client, your solicitor may contact that person direct, although usually he should, as a matter of courtesy, inform the other party's solicitor of his

intention to do so. This rule of professional etiquette does not prevent you from contacting the other party direct, a course often recommended by solicitors with a view to reaching a settlement. Nor does it affect the service of documents on the other party or the obtaining of a witness statement, as "there is no property in a witness". Nor do these principles prevent your solicitor from asking the Legal Aid Board to reconsider whether your opponent should have legal aid.

Misconduct by other solicitors
Your solicitor is also under a duty to report the misconduct of another solicitor (whether on the other side or in his own firm), to the Office for the Supervision of Solicitors. He may in certain circumstances have to seek your consent: 19.03.

Payment of fees
As your solicitor is personally responsible for paying the proper costs or fees (known as "disbursements") of professional agents, e.g. barristers, medical and other consultants, enquiry agents, engineers, surveyors and other experts, it is quite normal for him to insist on payment on account from you before carrying out any further work, even though he may not have sought any money on account of his own costs from you or billed you: 20.01. This applies also to foreign lawyers' fees: 20.02.

Unless you are legally aided, in which case the Legal Aid Board is responsible direct to counsel, your solicitor is personally liable to pay counsel's fees 20.06; he therefore has your implied authority to query counsel's fees as to their reasonableness.

Attendance at court
Since your solicitor is under a duty properly to instruct counsel or any other advocate: 20.03 and to attend on him in court: 20.04, this may well result in you receiving a larger bill from your solicitors than you might in theory expect. There are, however, instances e.g. in a magistrates or crown court, where it is unnecessary for your solicitor to attend subject only to your own interests and the interests of justice not being prejudiced:

20.04. First, you should not be offended if your solicitor does not come to the magistrates court, for example, on a committal to the Crown Court or an application for an adjournment; he will simply be saving you or the Legal Aid Board costs, knowing that you will be adequately represented. On the other hand, he may often be under a duty to counsel or the court to attend, even where it appears to you that his attendance is unnecessary or adds little to the proceedings. He is likely to attend, regardless of the circumstances, where witnesses other than character witnesses have to attend or, most importantly, if he anticipates that you might be sent to prison. He should always inform you that he does not intend to go to court and should also tell you your barrister's name.

Instructing counsel
Even where he has instructed counsel, your solicitor remains responsible to you: 20.05. Thus your solicitor is under a duty to apply his mind to your barrister's advice or opinion and consider its contents on their merits. He should check that your barrister has properly understood your case and not made any obvious mistakes of fact or gross errors of judgment, however eminent that counsel may be. Failure to do so could constitute professional negligence.

(j) Undertakings

Undertakings are important because they may affect your interests in money, property or the conduct of litigation.

Meaning
An undertaking is an unequivocal declaration of intention to another person with a view to reliance being placed on it and it may be made by a solicitor or member of his staff in the course of practice or, if not made in the course of practice, by a solicitor in his capacity as a solicitor: 18.01.

It is a binding promise to do or not to do something and may be written or oral. It is unnecessary for the word "undertake" to be used. If oral, it may be difficult to prove. If, however, it is confirmed in writing by the person to whom it has been made and not reasonably promptly repudiated or denied, then, unlike a contractual offer, which is greeted with silence, it would be deemed to have been confirmed or accepted.

Solicitors undertakings are commonly used in conveyancing: 25.11 and in particular for exchanging contracts, where there is a Code of Practice.

Implied undertakings
Certain undertakings are implied, whether as a matter of law or trade usage i.e. obligations of the profession. If your solicitor is sent a document or money subject to an express condition, he must return it if he is unwilling or unable to comply with the condition. If your solicitor is sent, say a cheque to be held to the order of the sender, he must not present it without consent. Where he asks for copies of documents, he impliedly agrees to pay the reasonable copying charges. If he has to stop a Client Account cheque, he must inform the payee promptly that he has done so.

Liability for an undertaking
Your solicitor does not have to give or accept an undertaking: 18.02. He can be liable for an undertaking even if the performance of it is not within his own control: 18.03. Thus it is no defence for him to say that a third party failed to do something he should have done or that his Client prevented him from performing his undertaking by terminating the retainer. The solicitor remains personally liable on his undertaking. If the undertaking relates to payment of money and the solicitor lacks the means, payment may be made on his behalf by the Solicitors' Indemnity Fund.

Dishonouring an undertaking is professional misconduct: 18.05. An undertaking only ceases on performance, court order or, most usually, release by the person to whom it was given. The Law Society (or its Council) will not become involved, if the performance of the undertaking is dependent on a point of law, which is disputed, or if it has been procured by fraud, deceit or innocent misrepresentation.

Changing solicitors
If your solicitor receives an undertaking for your benefit and you change solicitors, the benefit of the undertaking remains with you: 18.06. On the other hand, the burden or performance of the undertaking cannot be assigned or passed onto another solicitor without the approval of you or that solicitor. If a solicitor takes over the practice of a solicitor who gave the undertaking, the latter will remain liable, unless released, but the former will not become liable unless he expressly or by necessary implication adopts the undertaking.

Ambiguous undertakings
An undertaking "to use best endeavours" is unwise as it is open to argument. Where an undertaking is ambiguous, it is invariably construed in favour of the recipient: 18.07.

Consideration
Unlike a contract, there need be no consideration for an undertaking, although, if there is and it fails, the undertaking is automatically discharged. Your solicitor's undertaking on your behalf is binding on him even if given without your authority: 18.09, although this must be distinguished from your solicitor's statement of your assumed intentions.

Effect on the firm's partners
Your solicitor's undertaking also binds his partners (even if one of the partners leaves the firm) but not an incoming partner: 18.10.

Your solicitor or his firm is responsible for an undertaking given by any member of his firm, whether or not that person is a solicitor: 18.11.

Most importantly, your solicitor's undertaking binds you!
In view of all of the above, your solicitor would be unwise to give an undertaking without your express or implied authority and, furthermore, he may be liable to you in negligence for performance of an undertaking that results in you sustaining a loss: 18.13. Consequently, once you have been asked to give your solicitor written instructions, have done so and

such instructions have been acted on by your solicitor so that he might become liable, you may not revoke your instructions.

If your solicitor gives an undertaking dependent on a future event, he must notify the recipient so soon as it is clear the future event will not occur:

Generally an undertaking will stand or fall on its own wording: 18.15, although an undertaking to pay costs means "proper costs". This could lead to a detailed assessment of costs in the event that they are another solicitor's or party's costs. An undertaking to pay the costs of another professional, may well be dependent on whether the latter's profession can determine what costs are reasonable. One implication permitted is in the case of an undertaking to pay money out of a fund. In this case it is implied that the fund will be sufficient. It will not, however, be implied that an undertaking to pay a third party out of the proceeds of sale of your asset or property means out of the net proceeds of sale thereof. Therefore the solicitor should specify any prior deductions e.g. profit costs and agents' commission.

Enforcement
Finally, as your solicitor is an officer of the Court, the Court can enforce your solicitor's undertaking and, if it does so, the Council (of the Law Society) will not take disciplinary proceedings.

(k) Litigation and Advocacy; Misleading the Court

Your solicitor should as early as possible advise you as to whether, in view of the limitations of his own experience or expertise or practical considerations like his firm's limited facilities, your interests would be best served by another firm or the retaining of counsel: 21.03 Practice Rule 16B (choice of advocate).

As has already been said, your solicitor, whilst doing his best for you, must never deceive or mislead the court: 21.07. Not informing the judge of a case or provision, which might assist the other party, is a breach of this

PART TWO YOU WITH YOUR SOLICITOR

duty. His duty, however, does not extend to informing the other side or the court of the existence of a fact or witness, who could prejudice your own case.

The commonest question asked of lawyers is: "How can you defend someone you know to be guilty?" One of the ways in which the question is misleading is the equating of belief with knowledge. Unless the client tells the solicitor that he is guilty, then the lawyer never knows whether or not the client is guilty; the lawyer's personal belief (which should remain private and unspoken) is irrelevant. The question of guilt is a decision for the jury or court and not the lawyer. The main purpose of being represented by a lawyer is so that the client's best interests will be protected. Even guilty people have rights. Whatever his belief, this is his overriding professional duty, the only restriction on which is not knowingly to allow you to give false evidence or to call a witness, whose evidence is untrue. If you tell him you have "done it" and then insist on pleading "not guilty" he will be severely hampered in his task of defending you.

You would of course not be giving false evidence simply because you change your plea of "guilty" to "not guilty" or where you may have admitted to your solicitor that you made an oral or written "confession" of guilt to the police or any other witness. Your solicitor is governed by what you tell him; those are your instructions. Your so called confession, which will have to be contested and put by your solicitor to the witness, may be accounted for by any one of a number of explanations, e.g. that it was a matter of convenience at the time, you misunderstood the question or allegation, you were not feeling well or - very frequently - that your statement or confession was not voluntary in that it was induced by fear or a promise of favourable treatment. What matters is your account to your solicitor, however incredible. On the other hand, your solicitor would be failing in his duty, if he omitted to advise you that in his opinion, your story, account or explanation is incredible and therefore not likely to be accepted by the court or jury but once he has given that advice, if he then chooses to do so, he is obliged to carry out your instructions by putting your case, regardless of his personal belief.

The most extreme situation is reached where you have "confessed" to your own solicitor but nevertheless informed him that you intend, as is your right, to plead not guilty. He is still able to represent you and should do so to the best of his ability, although he will have to perform this delicate and difficult task with one arm tied behind his back. The restrictions in practice mean that (a) he can only seek to destroy the prosecution case by cross- examination, (b) he cannot risk calling you to give evidence lest you be cross examined and falsely deny the very guilt, of which you have informed him, and (c) he cannot call any witness to say anything, which he knows would be inconsistent with your guilt, e.g. an alibi witness, who is a witness, who says that you were not at the scene of the crime and therefore could not have committed it. In such circumstances, the best advice he could give you is to explain the restrictions on his personal professional position and "recommend" you to instruct another solicitor.

A notable example of misleading the court occurred in November 1987 when a solicitor, a Mr Bridgwood, was convicted in the Crown Court of acting in a manner tending and intending to pervert the course of public justice and was sentenced to nine months' imprisonment suspended for two years. He was later fined £2,000 by the Solicitors' Disciplinary Tribunal. What he had done was to make a plea in mitigation for his client without referring to her assumed name or her character, when, to his knowledge, she had pleaded guilty in a false name. He had previously advised her to reveal her true identity to the police, if only because it would be established through finger print evidence. Obviously this did not arise, when she pleaded guilty.

Apparently your solicitor need not correct false information given to the court by the prosecution or another party provided he himself does not actively participate in misleading the court by adopting the information.
If you give a false name, address or date of birth, this will mislead the

court, may affect the administration of justice from the point of view of bail and communication and prevent the police from ascertaining any previous convictions. If you ask your solicitor to subscribe to these inaccuracies, he is bound to cease to act for you. Although he may have to inform the court that he has ceased to act for you, he must not divulge his reason.

Surprisingly the only exception to an advocate not having to believe his client occurs in civil, not criminal, proceedings. If you instruct your solicitor to make an allegation of fraud on your behalf, he (and counsel) must satisfy himself (or themselves) that there is prima facie evidence of fraud.

(l) Witnesses

One of your solicitor's most important functions may well be the interviewing of witnesses.

As "there is no property in a witness", "witness" includes a person who may be expected to be - or even has been - called to give evidence by the other party. To avoid a charge of tampering with a witness, it may be prudent for your solicitor to interview such a witness with the other party's representative being present.

Despite the "comment" in The Guide to Professional Conduct of solicitors: 21.10 note 5 your solicitor should not advise a witness that he need not make a statement, as it is the witness's moral, if not legal, duty to assist the cause of justice. Once a witness has started to give evidence, he may not be spoken to about the case by anyone without either the leave of the court or the other party's consent until he has finished giving evidence: 21.10 note 6.

Your solicitor must not "reward" witnesses but must pay their expenses and may compensate them for loss of time: 21.11; he must of course pay an expert witness's reasonable fee. As your solicitor cannot obtain prior authority from the Legal Aid Board for the fees of experts in criminal cases, he is entitled to disclaim liability for fees disallowed on taxation or assessment in part or in full: 21.11 note 3.

As your solicitor cannot be both your advocate and witness, he should consider at the outset whether or not to accept your instructions or, even during the course of his retainer, stop acting for you, if he is likely to have to give evidence, unless his evidence is purely formal: 21.12. Alternatively, he may act, provided he instructs counsel. If it is clear at the outset that his evidence will be other than purely formal, two other factors arise. First, would advising you to retain another solicitor save unnecessary counsel's fees? Secondly, would the thought that your own solicitor's evidence might be viewed as not disinterested adversely affect your prospects of success?

(m) Commission and Interest

(i) Commission
During the course of his retainer, your solicitor may receive commissions on life policies, stocks and shares, pensions and general insurances such as household contents and fire policies (including renewals). As these commissions will have been received by him as your agent, he must pay them over to you, unless you consent to him keeping them. If the commission exceeds £20, he should tell you either the amount or the basis of its calculation and approximate amount. If it proves to be "materially in excess" of the original figure, he must account to you for the excess, even if you have already agreed to him keeping it.

14.14 states:"(1) Solicitors shall account to their clients for any commission received of more than £20 unless, having disclosed to the client in writing the amount or basis of calculation of the commission or (if the precise amount or basis cannot be ascertained) an approximation thereof, they have the client's agreement to retain it.

(2) Where the commission actually received is materially in excess of the amount or basis or approximation disclosed to the client, the solicitor shall account to the client for the excess."

Less than £20 is "de minimis" (i.e., so small that it may be disregarded) but the rule would apply, if the totality of a number of small commissions exceeded £20. The wise solicitor will therefore obtain your consent before he receives the commission(s).Unless your commission has been earmarked for paying other disbursements, he may use it towards paying your bill. Taking your commission in part payment of his bill to you is in fact beneficial to you because he need only levy VAT on the balance due: note 15.

(ii) Interest
When money is paid by you to your solicitor on account or received by him on your behalf, you may be entitled, subject to time for clearance of cheques, to interest. Whether or not interest is payable is dependent on the amount being held and the time for which it is held. The rules are laid down in Part III of the Solicitors' Accounts Rules 1991. The minimum amount is £1000 held for eight weeks up to £20,000 held for more than one week but interest may be payable on more than £20,000, even though held for less than a week: 28.25. The rules have been made pursuant to s.33. The rate of interest will usually be dependent on the rate of interest at the solicitor's bank. In the case of very large sums, your solicitor may be under a duty to hold your money in a separate designated account so that the amount of interest is maximised.

You and your solicitor may agree in writing to waive entitlement to interest: 28.31 and Rule 26(a) of the Solicitors' Accounts Rules but not if he is a trustee because that would be a breach of the fundamental legal rule that "A trustee may not benefit from his trust": 28.32.

A solicitor, who is a stakeholder, must pay the interest earned to the ultimate payee of the stake: 25.15.

A STRAIGHTFORWARD GUIDE TO YOU AND YOUR SOLICITOR

The Interest Rules

Rule 20: Subject to Rule 26 your solicitor must account to you for interest in accordance with rule 21.

Rule 21: He must pay you interest where he holds -

- (i) £1,000 for more than eight weeks
£2,000 for more than four weeks
£10,000 for more than two weeks
£20,000 for more than one week or

- (ii) more than £20,000 for less than one week when it would be fair and reasonable to account to you for interest or

- (iii) "money continuously, which varies significantly in amount over the period during which it is held and it is fair and reasonable so to account having regard to any sum payable under paragraph (i) of this rule and to the varying amounts money and length of time for which these are held"; or

- (iv) money intermittently during the course of acting and it is fair and reasonable so to account having regard to all the circumstances including the aggregate of the sums held and the periods for which they are held notwithstanding that no individual sum would have attracted interest under paragraph (i) of this rule or;

- (v) where rule 22 applies.

Rule 22 deals with the special situation where the money is held in a separate designated account.

Rule 23 deals with the calculation of interest.

Rule 24 Subject to rule 26(c)... where your solicitor holds money as a stakeholder... he shall pay interest... to the person to whom the stake is paid.

Rule 25 Without prejudice to any other remedy...available, if you feel aggrieved that you have not received interest, you are "entitled to apply to the Law Society for a Certificate as to whether or not interest ought to have been earned" and, if so, its amount: and upon the issue of such a certificate the sum certified to be due shall be payable by the solicitor to the client.

Rule 26 Nothing in ... these rules shall:
(a) affect any arrangement in writing, whenever made, between you and your solicitor as to the application of your money or interest thereon;
(b) apply to money received by your solicitor, which is subject to a controlled trust or received by him as the trustee rather than as solicitor;
(c) "affect any agreement in writing for payment of interest on stake holder money held by a solicitor."

If your solicitor gives you a bill and provided he has given you notice of your rights and remedies, interest will start to run a month after delivery of the bill on whatever amount is found to be outstanding: 14.11.

"In a contentious matter, a solicitor may charge interest on an unpaid bill:

(a) If the right to charge interest has been expressly reserved in the original retainer agreement or

(b) If a Client has later agreed to pay it for a contractual consideration or

(c) Where the Solicitor has sued the client and claimed interest under Section 35A of the Supreme Court Act 1981.": 14.12.

Solicitors Act sections referred to: 33. The relevant Solicitors' Accounts Rules are rules 20 to 26, which are set out in full in Appendix 2.

(n) Changing Your Solicitor

Whereas you may change your solicitor at any time by terminating his retainer with or without good reason, he may only cease acting for you for good reason: see (a) The Retainer.

Like all relationships, that between you and your solicitor may suffer an irretrievable breakdown! This could occur for a number of reasons. You may be unable to afford his charges, feel that he is too slow, find him negligent or incompetent, have no faith in him or simply dislike him!

Provided you have paid his bill, you are entitled to receive all your papers, apart from those documents which are his property, a topic which is also dealt with under (o) Termination of Retainer.

Legally aided clients
If, however, you are legally aided, you have to provide a good reason for changing your solicitor. By regulation 51(f) of the Civil Legal Aid (General) Regulations 1989 the Area Director may amend a certificate where in his opinion a change of solicitor should be authorised. Usually it is quite sufficient for there simply to have been a loss of confidence and, although your solicitor must give his consent, he is usually only too willing to forward your request and reason and simultaneously consent to there being a transfer, in which case he will send your papers to your new (successor) solicitor. Sometimes, however, where a lot of work has already been done, the Legal Aid Board may be unwilling to authorise a transfer, especially if your solicitor objects. The Legal Aid Board itself might object as your new solicitor would have to be remunerated for perusing the work of your previous solicitor, which would result in a waste of Legal Aid Board funds.

If, being legally aided, you change your solicitor, your papers cannot be sent to your new solicitor until the Legal Aid Certificate has been amended into your new solicitor's name by the Legal Aid Board, although the new solicitor may be allowed copies or sight of your papers in the meantime. As the solicitor's fees are secured by the legal aid certificate, he cannot demand an undertaking for his costs from your new solicitor, unless they are pre-certificate i.e. private costs.

Criminal proceedings
In criminal proceedings the application is usually made direct to the court. If the court thinks that you are being unreasonable, especially where a considerable amount of work has already been carried out and there would appear to be no good reason for a change of solicitor, the court could refuse a transfer. Obviously if your instructions have "embarrassed" your solicitor, a transfer will be made without difficulty.

(o) Termination of Retainer; Lien

When the retainer is terminated, you are entitled to a statement of account and the return of your papers and property: 12.11, subject only to your solicitor's lien (i.e. right to retain them) pending payment of his fees or costs: 12.12. Even his lien, however, can be circumvented by you (or the Law Society): s68.

What the client is entitled to on termination
Assuming there is no lien, on termination of the retainer, you are entitled to all documents held by your solicitor except his documents. This means that you are entitled to instructions and briefs to Counsel, attendance notes on third parties, copies of letters or documents made for your benefit, all documents that came into existence before the retainer, copies of letters to third parties, receipts and vouchers for disbursements made on your behalf, medical reports, witness statements, advices and opinions from Counsel, letters from third parties, pleadings, affidavits, court orders and other documents, such as requests and supplies of further (and better)

particulars but not to attendance notes, (i.e. his record of an attendance on you), copies of letters from him to you, spare copies of his letters to third parties, tape recordings of conversations, his internal memoranda, his diary entries, his timesheets and computer records, his books of account and your letters, authorities and instructions to him.

Joint retainers

If the solicitor has a joint retainer, he should not give you the originals of "your documents" without your fellow client's consent; each of you is, however, entitled to a copy at your own expense. If your solicitor has acted for your mortgagee, there may be certain documents of which, though yours, the mortgagee is entitled to have copies.

Keeping records after termination

After the matter is over, regardless of whether the retainer has been formally terminated, he should preserve your file for six years after the time when any possible cause of action could have arisen. Even though there is no longer value in the papers even after the six years have elapsed, and he should try to obtain your consent before destroying them.

Calculating the bill

Apart from being able to see your file, you are entitled to know how your bill has been arrived at; your solicitor's omission to do so may make him liable in negligence: 13.05. You are also entitled to a proper bill: s.68.

In conveyancing, if you do not pay your solicitor his proper costs, he has a lien over and may retain your title deeds until payment: 25.14. Thus this rule will only apply to you, as seller, if the sale aborts, or to you, as buyer, if the sale goes through; otherwise the title deeds would not be yours and no lien would arise. His lien can, however, be circumvented by you (or the Law Society): s.68.

Termination by the solicitor

Article 3 of the CCBE Code of Conduct for Lawyers in the EEC, which is headed "Relations with Clients", states:

3.1.4. A lawyer shall not be entitled to exercise his right to withdraw from a case in such a way or in such circumstances that the client may be unable to find other legal assistance in time to prevent prejudice being suffered by the client.

Your solicitor has a right to terminate his retainer on reasonable notice if he asks for a reasonable sum on account of costs and you refuse or fail to pay it within a reasonable time: s.65.

Solicitors Act sections referred to: 65 and 68.

PART III - YOU AGAINST YOUR SOLICITOR

(a) What remedies have you against your solicitor?

If you consider that your solicitor has acted improperly or unlawfully, overcharged you or acted negligently, you can

(a) complain to the Office for the Supervision of Solicitors, from which there is a right of appeal to the Legal Services Ombudsman;

(b) apply to the Solicitors Disciplinary Tribunal: ss 47(1) and 55 or to the High Court: ss.31, 51 and 55 to have him struck off or to require him to answer allegations contained in an affidavit;

(c) require your solicitor to obtain a remuneration certificate from the Office for the Supervision of Solicitors, who administer this process, pursuant to the Solicitors' (Non Contentious Business) Remuneration Order 1994 or apply to the High Court or the county court for your solicitor's bill of costs to be assessed in respect of work carried out both contentious and non-contentious business (even where there has already been a remuneration certificate) pursuant to ss 70-72;

(d) apply to the Law Society for a certificate of interest;

(e) cause him to be financially investigated;

(f) obtain an order that he delivers his bill and/or returns your papers to you;

(g) cause the Law Society to intervene in his practice; and/or

(h) sue him for professional negligence, fraud, money had and received, return of documents or other property or any such other appropriate remedy.

PART THREE YOU AGAINST YOUR SOLICITOR

All these rights and remedies are dealt with in greater detail in the ensuing sections.

If you believe that your solicitor has committed a crime e.g. theft of money, deeds or property, falsification of accounts, forgery, etc, you may report him to the police.

WARNING In the case of litigation it is essential to realise that none of the above courses of action apart from (h) itself will directly affect or advance your case. Consequently, if you chose to pursue any of the above remedies, you should also take steps to continue to prosecute your case personally or instruct another solicitor to do so on your behalf.

Solicitors Act sections referred to: 31, 47, 51, 55, 68, 70, 71 and 72.

(b) Complaint to the OSS

The Office for the Supervision of Solicitors ("OSS") was set up on 1 September 1996 to replace the Solicitors' Complaints Bureau, which had been heavily criticised for its delays and generally formal, legalistic and unsympathetic approach to clients and other members of the public. In response to these criticisms, the Law Society, which wished to retain the machinery of self-regulation, decided to rename the SCB accordingly. In so far as the OSS is basically staffed by the same personnel as was the SCB, only time will tell as to whether what many regard, somewhat cynically, as a public relations exercise will result in any improvement. It is fair to say, however, that the profession has purported to invite complaints and has made - and asked its solicitor members to make - leaflets available for clients informing them how they might complain.

The OSS, which is the Law Society's "independent complaints handling arm", deals with "a number of related regulatory matters". Its powers, which are derived from statute and the Society's Charter, have been delegated by the Council to the Compliance and Supervision Committee and to the OSS's Director and Assistant Directors pursuant to section

79(1). The Committee in turn delegates to various sub-committees: 30.01. Obviously you cannot complain to the OSS about the decision of the Legal Aid Board or a court order, giving judgment against you; nor will the OSS consider whether your solicitor's opinion on the law or advice on procedure and tactics has been correct; and the OSS certainly will not decide whether your solicitor has been negligent.

Apart from administering the remuneration certificate process, the OSS exists mainly to investigate whether or not your solicitor has been in breach of the rules of professional conduct and also to investigate the quality of professional service supplied to you by your solicitor. Initially it often refers complaints back to solicitors' firms' own complaints handling procedure as well as attempting to conciliate.

"Working for excellence and fairness" is the mission statement of the OSS, which has been endeavouring with some success to improve on the performance of its predecessor. Its Director, Peter Ross, recognises that "one of our most pressing priorities is to avoid delay and resolve complaints speedily." Although solicitors are represented, it claims that laymen constitute two thirds of the membership of its committees.

The OSS claims that "staff are trained to resolve a complaint through conciliation without resorting to a formal investigation, where this is possible and appropriate. Where matters are referred to case working teams, trained Customer Service Officers attached to each team provide on-the-spot information about the progress of a complaint or investigation, allowing case workers to focus on the investigation work itself."

You are therefore encouraged, where appropriate, to make your initial complaint to your solicitor or the person in his firm dealing with complaints. The OSS can investigate complaints about conduct from non-clients: 30.02, although, with regard to other solicitors, e.g. those acting for your opponent, your right to complain is far more limited. A real delay by the other party's solicitor may well be a legitimate, albeit immoral, tactic carried out for your opponent on his instructions; if so instructed by his client, such delay cannot be the subject of a complaint by you.

Your solicitor must deal promptly with letters from the OSS, in default of which he may be refused a practising certificate or have conditions attached to it: 30.04. He can be ordered to produce his files: s.44B. His failure to comply with a decision of the Compliance and Supervision Committee or one of its sub-committees can itself amount to professional misconduct: 30.04 note 3.

Your solicitor cannot exempt himself from investigation by the OSS and, if he tries to prevent a client from reporting him, this is itself unbefitting conduct: 30.03 note 2; nor may he seek compensation in consideration of not reporting an alleged breach of undertaking: 30.03 note 4.

Your solicitor cannot sue you for defamation in respect of a complaint because it is covered by qualified privilege, although such a defence may be rebutted by malice. Should your solicitor threaten this, this itself would be prima facie evidence of professional misconduct: 30.03 note 5.

Complaints frequently arise in probate work, where you, either as executor under a will or personal representative on an intestacy or as a beneficiary, have a "right" to complain but, unless your complaint is one of delay, the OSS will not investigate until after the estate has been wound up.

If you believe your solicitor may have been negligent, to which possibility he might himself have alerted you, you should immediately seek advice from another solicitor.

Should you feel that your complaint to the OSS is "getting nowhere fast", there is no reason why you should not apply to the SDT (see Part III (h) below) but you should ask the OSS to suspend its investigation. This is because the SDT, having held that it has no jurisdiction to adjudicate on an application made by the Law Society, where the OSS itself has already adjudicated, it is thought likely that the SDT would decline jurisdiction by way of consistency or analogy.

When considering a complaint that the service provided by your solicitor has been inadequate under s37A and paragraphs 1, 2 and 3 of Schedule 1A thereto, the OSS will look into such matters as delay, not providing you with proper estimates of your costs or exceeding an estimate, not keeping you properly informed of relevant matters, not answering your calls and letters and ignoring your instructions.

If your complaint is upheld, it is most likely that the OSS will -

(a) in the case of professional misconduct, admonish or rebuke your solicitor or, if they consider it more serious, exercise the Law Society's powers of intervention under Schedule 1 of the SA1974 and/or institute proceedings in the SDT;

(b) in the case of inadequate professional service, reduce your solicitors bill and/or require him to compensate you up to £1,000 and/or order him to rectify his mistake without charge.

According to the OSS's Annual Report for its first full year until September 1997, just over 90% of the complaints, where a first instance decision related to poor service, resulted in a finding in favour of the complainant. Over 45% of those complaints resulted in compensation, reduced costs or both. In over 9% there was no adverse finding.

According to the OSS's figures for January to December 1998, 95% of the complaints, where a first instance decision related to poor service, resulted in a finding in favour of the complainant. Over 80% of those complaints resulted in compensation, reduced costs or both. In just over 5% there was no adverse finding.

The OSS's Director, Peter Ross, has offered no explanation for the steep increase in the number of complaints, resulting in compensation, reduced

PART THREE YOU AGAINST YOUR SOLICITOR

costs or both, and has declined to comment on whether the situation will improve in the future.

If you are dissatisfied with the OSS's decision or manner, in which they handled your complaint, you have a right of appeal to the Legal Services Ombudsman.

The address of the OSS is Victoria Court 8 Dormer Place Leamington Spa Warwickshire, CV32 5AE telephone 01926 820082.

The powers of the OSS
For the purpose of making a complaint against your solicitor, the main powers of the OSS have been set out above. Several of its other powers have been set out elsewhere. It is, however, convenient to set out here a full list of its powers. The OSS may:

(a) rebuke for professional misconduct

(b) in the case of inadequate professional services under section 37 of the Solicitors Act and Schedule 1A thereto, disallow all or part of the costs, direct a solicitor to rectify an error, direct him to pay compensation up to £1,000 and direct him to take at his own expense such action in a client's interest as it may specify

(c) require interest to be paid under rule 25 of the Solicitors Accounts Rules 1991

(d) refuse to grant a practising certificate or grant one subject to conditions

(e) impose conditions on a current practising certificate under section 13A(1)

(f) suspend a solicitor's investment business certificate

(g) in the case of undue delay, appoint an agent to recover money and papers for a client or his new solicitor

(h)　　have a solicitor's accounts inspected

(i)　　disqualify a solicitor's accountant from giving a report

(j)　　intervene under Schedule 1 of the Solicitors Act

(k)　　institute disciplinary proceedings before the SDT

The OSS's powers under (c), (g), (j) and (k) are dealt with later in Part III.

How is a complaint made?
To make a complaint you may either (a) telephone the OSS and ask them to send you a "Complaint Referral Form" or (b) write to the OSS (see address above). Try to make your complaint as clear and concise as possible. Ideally you should state at the outset the conduct, of which you are complaining, preferably with a reference to the Solicitors Act section and/or principle from the Guide, which has been contravened. Secondly, you should set out the relevant facts and enclose any supporting documents. If your complaint is accepted, the OSS will write to you accordingly.

In many cases, where the "misconduct" is "minor", the OSS will probably endeavour to "conciliate" between you and your solicitor and bring about a satisfactory conclusion. In more serious cases, however, the OSS will set in motion its machinery for dealing with misconduct. It will invariably wish to pass on your complaint in full in order to invite the comments of the solicitor in question. You will then be given a right of reply.
Thereafter, the matter will be submitted in the form of a "case note" composed by one of the staff or "case workers" of the OSS. Eventually the matter will be put before the appropriate committee for its adjudication. Finally, there will be a right of appeal by either party to the OSS's own appeals committee; this follows a similar procedure. Only when the matter has been dealt with in that way, will you be allowed to

proceed, if so desired, with a complaint to the Legal Services Ombudsman.

Solicitors Act sections referred to: 13A(1), 37A, 44B and 79(1)

(c) The Legal Services Ombudsman

The Ombudsman was set up by the Courts and Legal Services Act 1990 to deal with complaints arising from the OSS (the General Council of the Bar and the General Council for Licensed Conveyancers). He is independent and his services are free. The Ombudsman may be contacted by telephone or letter. You have three months, in which to make your complaint about your solicitor, the OSS or both of them, starting from the time when you were informed of the decision of the OSS.

The Ombudsman's primary function is to investigate the manner, in which your complaint was handled by the OSS, for which he is in effect a "court of appeal", although he can reinvestigate your complaint ab initio, ie afresh. The Ombudsman cannot consider decisions of the court, the Solicitors' Disciplinary Tribunal, the Solicitors' Indemnity Fund or the Legal Aid Board.

The Legal Services Ombudsman, having obtained the file from the OSS, will do the following:

- take no further action,
- criticise the OSS but make no further recommendation,
- recommend the OSS to reconsider your complaint or use its disciplinary powers or
- recommend the OSS or your solicitor or both of them to pay compensation for any loss, inconvenience or distress, which you may have suffered.

The Ombudsman will always give reasons.

The culprit, whether solicitor or OSS, has three months to comply with any recommendation. Failure to do so will result in the Ombudsman publicising your complaint, which is invariably done in the local newspaper, and recovering the cost from the solicitor or OSS. This has had to be done on a few occasions.

According to the Ombudsman's Seventh Annual Report for 1997, of 1,519 investigations carried out, 1,332 (87.7%) concerned solicitors, in respect of 10% of whom formal criticism was made. Surprisingly, more than 25% resulted in some form of favourable action from the complainant's point of view, the Ombudsman recommending that the OSS should reconsider 100 cases, that the OSS should pay compensation in 101 cases and that the solicitor should pay compensation in 137 cases. The OSS duly complied but not all the solicitors complied. Of the 11 solicitors who failed to comply, seven had ceased to practise by the time of the recommendations. Three of the remainder rejected the recommendation to pay compensation and, as they were entitled to do, publicised their failure and the reason for it; a single solicitor failed to accept the recommendation or publicise the outcome with the consequence that the Ombudsman published a notice at the expense of the solicitor.

The current Ombudsman is Ann Abraham, who was appointed on 22 September 1997. She has a wide experience, having worked in local government in the Housing Corporation. She is currently a non-executive Director of the Benefits Agency, a member of the Bar Council's Pro Bono Unit Advisory Board and a member of the Director General for Fair Trading's Assessment Panel for the Excellence in Trading Standards Award. Immediately before her present appointment she was Chief Executive of the National Association of Citizens Advice Bureaux.

The address of the Legal Services Ombudsman is 22 Oxford Court Oxford Street Manchester M2 3WQ telephone 0161 236 9532.

(d) Delay and Negligence

(i) Delay

Unfortunately one of the three commonest complaints clients have against their solicitors (the others being lack of communication and over-charging or sending bills for far more than is expected) is delay. The main causes of delay by solicitors are sheer inefficiency, the taking on of too much work and poor health or nervous breakdown

At the very least your solicitor's delay may cause you stress or anxiety; in some circumstances delay may amount to inadequate professional service or professional negligence. In the first instance you should obviously try to speak to your solicitor and, if you do not hear from him as promised, follow it up with a suitable letter. Should your verbal and/or written complaint not produce the desired result, your best course - whatever other remedy you may pursue - is simply to seek to change solicitors. In the long run this will result in far less aggravation.

Undue delay
If he is guilty of undue delay, the Law Society has power to obtain possession of your papers and money paid on account and return them to you or to your new solicitor: paragraph 3 of Schedule 1 of the Solicitors Act 1974.

Avoidable delay
If he has been guilty of avoidable delay in litigation or gross misconduct or gross negligence, the court can make a wasted costs order or impose a penalty on him.

Inordinate and inexcusable delay
If your case is struck out for want of prosecution on the grounds of inordinate and inexcusable delay, you may well be able to sue him for damages for loss of your prospect of success.

(ii) Negligence

Apart from delay, your solicitor may be negligent by failing to give you proper advice.

Actions for professional negligence against solicitors are similar to actions for professional negligence against other professionals but, whereas in medical negligence the test is dependent on the then state of medical knowledge and accepted views as to treatment, in the case of professional negligence against solicitors (and barristers), one must really prove what may be described as "gross negligence". "Gross negligence" means something that is obviously wrong and not merely wrong in the opinion of other lawyers or wrong as borne out by the judgment of a court. In other words a mere piece of bad advice or wrong opinion does not necessarily form the basis for an action against a solicitor. It is no more than an error of judgment, which, for good or bad, is simply one of the hazards or misfortunes inherent in our legal system. One only has to reflect that it is possible for three judges to be "right" and six judges to be "wrong" to realise this. For example, you could win your case in the county court or High Court (one judge), win again in the Court of Appeal (three judges), if the other party appeals, and yet lose in the House of Lords (by a majority of three judges to two),thereby losing your case even though six out of nine judges agreed with you!

One example of negligent advice concerns the availability of legal aid. Your solicitor's failure to advise you of the availability of legal aid under the Legal Aid Act 1988, whereby you might be entitled to financial assistance, could amount to unbefitting conduct and negligence for breach of duty owed. His duty applies throughout the retainer so that, if, having instructed him privately, your financial circumstances deteriorate, you should inform him. If you become legally aided, he must still perform his work for you according to the same standard of care.

With regard to negligence, your solicitor will be liable in an action for damages for professional negligence if he carelessly either advises you on a particular course or omits to advise you on the correct course but, most importantly, he is not liable for not giving advice on aspects, which are outside the normal scope of the transaction, on which he has been instructed.

It is impossible to give a complete list of negligent acts or omissions. Common examples might include:-

Generally

(a) failing to explain the provisions of a deed, will, bill of sale, lease or mortgage;

(b) failing to draw up an agreement so as to include an obvious and essential term or failing to ensure that it is in the proper form or has been properly executed;

(c) misconstruing a clear contractual clause;

(d) not advising on the existence of a statutory provision;

(e) missing a time limit;

(f) carrying out unnecessary work;

Property

(a) acting without the authority of your spouse or other joint owner.

(b) when acting for a lessee, failing to ensure that the vendor has a good title or failing to obtain a copy of the head lease and proof that the rent has been paid;

(c) giving wrong advice on the covenants in a lease;

(d) leaving a vendor of property open to liability under an unusual covenant;

(e) failing to register an option to purchase;

(f) not advising a purchaser of a property that it is subject to some defect or incumbrance;

(g) failing to advise with regard to a tenancy, to which the land is subject;

(h) failing to advise a purchaser of the absence of planning permission for an existing erection or proposed building of a house; and

(i) failing to search the commons register in respect of vacant land;.

Your solicitor will not, however, be liable for not reminding you to terminate a lease, unless he has been specifically instructed to do so; nor will he be liable for failing to give your purchaser correct answers to preliminary enquiries before contract, which he should point out are your responsibility.

Wills

(a) where, having been instructed to prepare a will and knowing that it is urgent because the testator might suddenly die, he may be liable to intended beneficiaries if he fails to ensure that the will is duly attested before the testator's death;

(b) failing to ensure proper attestation of a will;

Litigation and other Contentious Matters

(a) failing properly to investigate a cause of action or defence;

(b) not instructing suitable counsel or failing to exercise his own mind on counsel's opinion or as to his advice; although this book is not concerned with barristers, it will be no defence for your solicitor to plead that he instructed counsel. Not only must he instruct a suitably experienced barrister - if necessary a specialist in the field - but also he must exercise his own mind on counsel's opinion or advice;

(c) advising you to start an action, if it is unlikely to succeed; but he is not negligent, if he reasonably believed that your instructions were correct or is specifically instructed to proceed even where he has explained that you are unlikely to succeed in your action or defence;

(d) failing to issue writ in time;

(e) bringing action in wrong court;

(f) allowing judgment by default, if defending;

(g) inexcusable delay;

(h) failing to obtain a witness statement;

(i) failing to follow the correct court procedure, whereby an order for paying the other party's costs is made;

(j) failing to inform you of an offer to settle;

(k) failing properly to prepare for trial or call a material witness;

(l) failing to attend a hearing;

(m) failing to enforce judgment; and

(n) failing to advise on appeal or the time limits for appealing.

Suing for professional negligence

If you do decide to sue your solicitor for professional negligence, there is no rule preventing another solicitor from acting for you. It is often believed that other solicitors will not sue a fellow solicitor. This is not true. It may, however, be sensible not to instruct a solicitor in the same neighbourhood as the proposed defendant or one who knows him or his firm. Having said this, there should be no difficulty in finding a suitable solicitor in the normal way. You may of course sue him yourself, in which case you will be a litigant in person. The law and procedure will be identical to that in most other ordinary types of civil action.

If you have a good case, you need not worry about whether your solicitor will be able to satisfy any judgment against him as he has to be insured: see Part I (e) by the Solicitors Indemnity Fund, who will invariably instruct one of the members of their own panel of solicitors to represent his firm.

A draft Statement of Case is included in Appendix 4. Further guidance on the procedure may be found in "Taking your own Legal Action" by this author.

(e) Remuneration Certificates and Detailed Assessment of Costs

On receipt of your solicitor's bill of costs, which will include any disbursements, you must either pay it or, if you consider it to be excessive, either require a remuneration certificate or apply for detailed assessment.

If you ignore your solicitor's bill, he will not unnaturally be entitled to sue you but must not do so without informing you in writing that you may have a right to require him to obtain a remuneration certificate for any non-contentious business or have his contentious costs assessed by a costs Judge or district judge. Once he has given you notice of your rights and remedies, interest will start to run a month after delivery of the bill on whatever amount is later found to be outstanding: 14.11.

Unless he believes that you are likely to evade justice by leaving the jurisdiction or dissipating your assets, he must wait a month before suing you:14.09 and s.69. In a non-contentious matter, you may have your solicitor's bill taxed in addition to or instead of obtaining a remuneration certificate. If your solicitor fails to meet your request to obtain a remuneration certificate, he may be disciplined for unprofessional conduct. He himself may apply for detailed assessment but primarily this is your responsibility. If someone else is paying your bill, that third party, having a legitimate interest, may apply for detailed assessment:14.09 and s71.

If your solicitor overcharges you, which is a matter of fact, either in his bill or for money on account, he is liable to disciplinary action on the ground that he sought to take unfair advantage of you, his client. If the remuneration certificate is for less than half the sum claimed, the relevant officer has to inform The Law Society. Even if the bill has been prepared for him by a specialist known as a "costs draftsman", the solicitor is still responsible for it: 14.13 note 4.

Your solicitor may render "a bill containing detailed items or a gross sum bill": s.64 (1). If you receive a gross sum bill you may demand a detailed bill within three months and prior to being sued, in which case the gross sum bill is of no effect s.64 (2). If you are sued on a gross sum bill, you have one month from service to apply for detailed assessment: s.64 (3) and the taxing officer himself may require details by way of breakdown or the formalised solicitor's bill of costs, which has three columns: s.64 (4). There is nothing to stop the detailed bill being higher than the gross sum bill but, if this be done, it must be done within the three month period unless you yourself choose to waive that particular right: Carlton v Theodore Goddard & Co (1973) 2 All ER 877. Even if you are only a beneficiary under a will being administered by a solicitor, you may in limited circumstances have the right to require a remuneration certification as you may be an "entitled person". Similarly if you are charged for the legal costs of your mortgage by your bank or building society.

If your cheque to your solicitor is dishonoured, although normally a person may sue on dishonour of a cheque without having to prove that any value has been given, he cannot use this form of action to circumvent your rights under the Solicitors Act.

(i) Remuneration Certificates

Remuneration certificates apply only to non-contentious work i.e. work other than litigation.

The Office for the Supervision of Solicitors ("OSS") is responsible for administering the Remuneration Certificate scheme for non-contentious work where your solicitor's profit costs are not more than £50,000. The current scheme is contained in the Solicitors' (Non-Contentious Business) Remuneration Order 1994 (S.I. 1994 No 2616), which was made pursuant to s.56 of the SA1974.

On being required to do so, your solicitor is obliged to apply for a certificate to the Remuneration Certificates Department of the OSS. The certificate obtained states what would be a "fair and reasonable charge" and it then becomes payable. The Remuneration Certificate procedure does not affect your right to have the bill taxed: 30.06.

If you consider that your solicitor's bill is too high, it is always worth asking him informally to justify and/or reduce his charges before taking any formal action. Should this fail, however, you should request him - preferably in writing - to obtain a remuneration certificate and ask him to confirm in writing that he has done so. This must be done within one month of your receipt of the bill or of the notification that he has deducted his costs from money held to your credit, unless he has consented to postpone the running of or waived the one month's time limit. Unless he has deducted his costs from money held to your credit, he must inform you in writing of your right to require a remuneration certificate. At the same time as you request that he apply, you must pay all the disbursements and VAT and also half of net costs (if not already deducted) unless he or the

PART THREE YOU AGAINST YOUR SOLICITOR

Council of the Law Society waives this particular requirement. These alternative pre-requisites are laid down by article 11(2) of the Order. The commencement of the one month's time limit is postponed until the application for a waiver of the requirement to pay 50% of the costs has been dealt with.

The Guide contains a recommended but non-compulsory form of wording to be given by your solicitor by way of notification as to your rights to remuneration and detailed assessment: Annex 14D. It is sufficient for him to inform you that, subject to paying the disbursements, VAT and half the costs, you may require him to have his bill assessed under the remuneration order procedure and/or be entitled to have his charges assessed by the court in accordance with Sections 70-72. It is unnecessary for him further to explain these provisions or the procedure.

The remuneration certificate procedure is itself strange, if not unique, in that it is run by an associated and therefore non-independent arm of the Law Society's Council, i.e. the OSS, although the officials, who deal with remuneration and are experienced in it, are required to perform a quasi-judicial function.

As to the procedure itself, you will hear from the relevant OSS department with a request for information and comments. The taxing officer is required to take into account, when considering what is "fair and reasonable", all circumstances of the matter and work involved with particular attention to its complexity, difficulty or novelty, the skill, specialised knowledge and responsibility involved, the time spent on the work, the number and significance of any documents, the place and circumstances of the business, the value of the matter, whether any land is registered or unregistered (which is more difficult to deal with), the importance of the matter to you and any necessary approvals by other parties, such as residuary beneficiaries.

Were the taxing officer to certify that less than half of the amount claimed was fair and reasonable, this would mean that your solicitor had overcharged by more than 100%, which would amount to prima facie evidence of misconduct and be automatically reported to the professional conduct department of the OSS.

You will lose your right to require a remuneration certificate, (a) after you have paid his bill other than by deduction, (b) one month after the bill has been delivered and you have been notified of your right to remuneration/detailed assessment, (c) if you made a non-contentious business agreement, (d) if an order for detailed assessment is made or, (e) "if article 11 (2) applies": Article 9.

The relevant passages of the Solicitors (Non-Contentious Business) Remuneration Order 1994 may be summarised as follows:

Interpretation

Article 2. In this Order-
"costs" means the amount charged in a solicitor's bill, exclusive of disbursements and VAT.

"entitled third party" means a residuary beneficiary....

Article 3. A solicitor's costs shall be such sum as may be fair and reasonable to both solicitor and entitled person, having regard to all the circumstances of the case and in particular to-

   (a) the complexity of the matter or the difficulty or novelty of the questions raised;

   (b) the skill, labour, specialised knowledge and responsibility involved;

   (c) the time spent on the business;

(d) the number and importance of the documents prepared or perused, without regard to length;

(e) the place where and the circumstances in which the business or any part thereof is transacted;

(f) the amount or value of any money or property involved;

(g) whether any land involved is registered land;

(h) the importance of the matter to the client; and

(i) the approval (express or implied) of the entitled person or the express approval of the testator to:-

    (i) the solicitor undertaking all or any part of the work giving rise to the costs or

    (ii) the amount of the costs.

Article 5. If less than half the costs are allowed, it must be reported to the Council of The Law Society.

Article 9. A client cannot require a remuneration certificate:

(a) after payment of a bill other than by deduction;

(b) after one month from the time when the bill was delivered and he has been notified of his right to remuneration/detailed assessment;

(c) after making a non-contentious business agreement;

(d) after an order for detailed assessment; or

(e) if Article 11 (2) applies (requirement to pay a sum towards the costs).

Article 11(1) On requesting a remuneration certificate you must pay your solicitor all disbursements paid by him and VAT plus 50% of a profit costs unless (a) you have already paid them by deduction or (b) the solicitor or the Council has agreed to waive all or part of this requirement.

(2) You must comply with (1) i.e. payment or application for waiver within one month or make payment within one month of refusal of waiver.

(ii) Detailed assessment

Detailed assessment is the judicial method of deciding on the fairness of your solicitor's costs. The detailed assessment procedure applies to all legal work, whether contentious or non-contentious, carried out by your solicitor in his capacity as solicitor. On detailed assessment the issues are whether or not an item of work was justified and, if so, the appropriate rate of payment, which might be less than the agreed rate.

If, however, you deny that there was ever a retainer, you must bring an action. There is, however, a difference between denying the existence of a retainer and disputing the authority for the carrying out of particular items of work, which latter may be done on a detailed assessment. On the other hand, if your solicitor applies for and obtains an order for detailed assessment, you can object to the whole bill on the ground of want of retainer, provided you have made no admission.

There are four different situations relating to detailed assessment.

(a) If you, as the party chargeable with the bill, apply to the court within one calendar month of the delivery of the bill, the court must order the bill to be assessed without any sum having to be paid into court or on account; until detailed assessment has been completed, you cannot be sued by your solicitor: s.70(1).

(b) If you apply to the court after one calendar month, the court may order the bill to be assessed and it may also order that no action against you be commenced or, if it has been, that it be stayed: s.70(2).

(c) Unless there are "special circumstances" you will lose the right to obtain detailed assessment if (i) twelve months have elapsed since delivery of the bill, (ii) judgment has already been given against you or (iii) the bill has been paid; in these circumstances, the court may impose conditions as to the costs of the assessment: s.70(3).

(d) Finally, you lose the right to apply for detailed assessment completely twelve months after payment of the bill: s.70(4).

Other persons may also apply for detailed assessment. In the case of a joint retainer, a single party may, as a party chargeable, apply for detailed assessment. The benefit of the right to apply for detailed assessment is also extended to a person other than "the party chargeable" if he is liable to pay it: s.71(1). This category includes trustees in bankruptcy, liquidators of companies and, importantly, lessees, who have to pay their lessors' costs, and beneficiaries under a trust, but it does not apply to someone, who voluntarily pays the costs.

If your solicitor's bill is unsigned, provided it has been delivered, it may still be assessed and paid and is sufficiently effective not to be capable of being withdrawn without leave.

It does not matter if the bill was wrongly addressed. Once delivered it cannot be substituted (i.e. replaced) by a new bill without your consent or leave of the court, although mathematical errors can be simply corrected on assessment.

In special circumstances a third party may apply for detailed assessment, when the bill has already been assessed: s.71(6). The third party applicant may also be able to show special circumstances, which the party chargeable could not do: s.71(2).

Any previously inherent jurisdiction of the court to order detailed assessment of a bill of costs at any time has been displaced by s.74: Harrison v Tew (1990) 2WLR 210 HL.

With regard to the expiration of the twelve month period, the time starts to run from the delivery of the final bill, which includes the last of a series of interim bills. With regard to the meaning of payment in (c)(iii) above this cannot take place before the bill has been delivered.

The "special circumstances" in s.70(3) cannot be fully categorised but have been defined as being "those which appear to the judge exercising such discretion so special and exceptional as to justify assessment". There does not have to be any misconduct or fraud. If you can show that any overcharging has taken place or that a charge appears to be unreasonably large or call for an explanation or that there are gross blunders or that your solicitor has reserved the right to deliver a further bill, all these can amount to special circumstances.

You cannot use the detailed assessment procedure as a mere delaying tactic because the court will invariably direct that any order for taxation shall automatically lapse, unless you apply for an appointment for taxation within say 14 days. Furthermore, interest will accrue on the amount ultimately found to be payable from the date when the bill was delivered.

For the purpose of detailed assessments "costs" comprises profit costs and disbursements. "Profit costs" means "costs other than counsel's fees or costs paid or payable in the discharge of a liability incurred by the solicitor on behalf of the party chargeable": s.70(12). Costs other than profit costs are generally known as disbursements.

An order for detailed assessment need not cover all the costs but may be limited to profit costs or disbursements and, if so limited, the result would be that your solicitor could start or continue to sue you for such costs as are not covered by the order: s.70(5) and (6).

Applications for detailed assessment are started by application under part 8 of the civil Procedure Rules, using form N208. Provided you have been duly notified, the detailed assessment hearing may proceed in your absence.

On detailed assessment, the taxing officer may (a) award interest on money wrongfully retained by your solicitor and (b) have regard to your solicitor's skill, labour and responsibility: s 66. It is curious that these two simple but different provisions are contained in one section of the Act.

The costs of the detailed assessment itself are dealt with at the end of the hearing: s.70(7) by way of summary assessment.

Obviously any reduction in your bill will be a bonus but it could be a Pyrrhic victory if the sum saved is less than the costs of the detailed assessment itself. If you succeed in reducing the amount of your solicitor's bill by one fifth, your solicitor will have to pay the costs of the detailed assessment unless (a) he applied for the detailed assessment and you did not attend or (b) the taxing officer certifies that there were "special circumstances": s.70(9) and (10). The one fifth rule relates to all costs, including disbursements, even if the latter have been paid, but VAT is not included. S.71(3) applies to trustees, executors and administrators.

According to the Guide, which does not have the force of law, although section 61 requires leave for an action on a contentious business agreement, that issue will be decided by the Court without any specific form of application prior to the issue of proceedings. Exceptionally your solicitor does not have to inform you of your right to apply for taxation, when suing you on a contentious business agreement: 14.10.

Under s.61 neither you nor your solicitor may sue on a contentious business agreement but an application may be made to a costs judge or district judge to enforce or set it aside, decide whether it is lawful or construe its terms: s.61(1), the main issue being whether it is unfair or unreasonable: s.61(4) just as, under s.57 (6) and (7), the costs judge or district judge may inquire into the number of hours worked and whether this was excessive: s.61(4A) and (4B).

The fact that the assessing officer has "passed" the agreement does not prevent the agreement from being set aside under s.61 (1) or re-opened under s.61 (5). Despite s.60(1) and despite your solicitor having been paid by you or someone on your behalf, you still have at least 12 months to apply to the Court for detailed assessment of the costs covered by the agreement: s.61(5). Your application may be brought in the appropriate county court, or if under the agreement you owe more than £50, the High Court: s.61(6). Applications are made under part 8 (see above)

S.72 "Supplementary provisions as to taxations" [i.e. detailed assessments] is extremely unlikely to be relevant; s.73 enables charging orders to be made pursuant to taxations; and s.74 "Special provisions as to contentious business done in County Court" broadly applies ss.59-73 to County Court work.

Solicitors Act sections referred to:56, 61, 66, 67, 68, 69, 70, 71, 72, 73 74.

Note: With the commencement of the Civil Procedure rules on 26th April 1999, the terminology with regards to costs changed but the actual Solicitors Act has not been amended. You should therefore understand all references in the Act to " Taxing Master/Officer", :taxing" or :taxation: to mean "costs judge/district judge', "assessing" or "detailed assessment: respectively.

(f) Certificate as to interest

If you know or discover that your solicitor has been holding money from you, whether it was received by him from you on account of costs and/or disbursements or received by him from any other person, and you consider that it should have earned interest for your benefit, you should politely raise this matter with him. He is under a duty to account to you for interest in many circumstances. Should you be dissatisfied with the outcome and/or fail to receive any interest, you have another remedy.

Under rule 25 you may apply to the OSS for a certificate stating whether interest ought to have been earned for you under the Solicitors Accounts Rules and, if so, the amount payable to you: 28.30.

(g) Financial Investigation

Should you have cause to suspect that all is not right with your client's account, you may so inform the Law Society, who, without divulging your communication, will send one of their investigating accountants to inspect your solicitor's accounts generally; they also have power, which they apparently often exercise, to do this at random: 28.33 and rule 27 of the Solicitor's Accounts Rules.

By rule 27(1) the Council of the Law Society has power to require your solicitor, in whichever capacity he has been acting, to produce his records and books of accounts for inspection with a view to there being a report on the result of such inspections. Such report may constitute the basis for proceedings under the Solicitors Act. This power may be exercised pursuant to "a written complaint lodged with them by a third party": rule 27(1)(c).

"Before instituting an inspection on a written complaint lodged" by you, "the Council shall require prima facie evidence that a ground of complaint exists, and may require the payment...of a reasonable sum...to cover the costs of the inspection and the costs of the solicitor against whom the complaint is made": rule 27(4).

(h) The Solicitors' Disciplinary Tribunal

The SDT, set up under s.46, comprises 24 members (16 solicitors and 8 laymen), who are appointed by the Master of the Rolls (MR). Each tribunal consists of three members, two solicitors admitted for more than 10 years, and one lay member: 31.01.

It has its own rules, approved by the MR. It is there to consider unbefitting conduct or breaches of the rules of professional conduct by solicitors, former solicitors, solicitor's clerks, former clerks and registered foreign lawyers. Section 46 deals with constitution and procedure. Section 47 deals with jurisdiction and the types of application and order that may be made.

By s.31(2) anyone may apply to the SDT, which, if satisfied that there is a prima facie case, will fix a hearing date: 31.02.

The SDT's rules are called the "Solicitors (Disciplinary Proceedings) Rules 1994" (S.I.No.288) and may be obtained from the SDT. The SDT sits at 60 Carey Street, which is round the corner from the Law Society and is also the home of the President of the Law Society during his tenure of office.

As in court, you may act for yourself, be represented, call witnesses and give evidence on oath or by affidavit: 31.03. Although the procedure is civil, the standard of proof is that required by the criminal courts, i.e. to be sure beyond a reasonable doubt as opposed to on the balance of probabilities.

The primary function of the SDT is neither to punish nor to compensate, which are the province of criminal and civil proceedings respectively, but to regulate the profession, maintain its good name and reputation and protect the public.

Unbefitting conduct
Although it is unlikely to have to do so, the SDT can make an order to enforce an award for inadequate professional services. It is mainly, however, concerned with "conduct unbefitting a solicitor" arising from a breach of professional rules of practice. The principles to be found in the Guide to Professional Conduct of Solicitors are not "law" but, as stated, a guide. Thus a breach may, not necessarily will, constitute unbefitting conduct. A breach of the professional rules is, however, prima facie evidence of misconduct.

What is "unbefitting conduct" is open to interpretation by the SDT. Mere negligence is probably insufficient but "gross" negligence would almost certainly be unbefitting conduct. In 1972 Lord Denning, MR said that the misconduct proved had to be "disgraceful or dishonourable" or "such as to be regarded as deplorable by his fellows in the profession". Obviously the profession changes its views as times themselves change.

The current definition is that laid down by the previous MR, Sir Thomas Bingham, now the Lord Chief Justice, who, in Ridehalgh v Horsefield (1994) 3All ER 648 said:

"Conduct which would be regarded as improper according to the consensus of professional, including judicial, opinion could be fairly stigmatised as such whether it violated the letter of a professional code or not."

It would thus appear that it is now easier to prove unbefitting conduct than it was in the days of Lord Denning. A conviction is usually unbefitting conduct but the SDT will not go behind a conviction save in exceptional circumstances. The SDT sometimes goes behind a civil decision. A solicitor can be struck off even where there is no finding of dishonesty.

Procedure
Should you wish to take your solicitor to the SDT, you should commence with an originating application supported by a statement of allegations and

summary of facts pursuant to rule 4 of the 1994 Rules. The statement is like a pleading. A solicitor member of the tribunal will decide if there is a prima facie case. Once made an application cannot be withdrawn without the consent of the SDT. Although there is no time limit, an application can be dismissed for inordinate delay. The SDT announces its order after the hearing and delivers written reasons later.

The SDT has for some several years been open to the public, although interlocutory proceedings, e.g. pre-trial reviews and other applications and matters, where a successful application for the hearing to be held in private has been made, will not be open to the public.

Powers of the SDT
The SDT may

(a) dismiss the application,
(b) strike off,
(c) suspend indefinitely or for a specified time,
(d) fine up to £5,000 per allegation,
(e) exclude from legal aid permanently or for a specified time and
(f) order costs or a contribution to be paid: 31.05.

The SDT's powers relating to registered foreign lawyers are set out in Schedule 14 paragraph 15 of the Courts and Legal Services Act 1990. A foreign lawyer may be struck off the register, suspended or fined.

Solicitors' clerks
Under section 43 the Society may apply to the SDT in respect of a solicitor's clerk: 31.08. In effect there are similar punishments for clerks.

Appeals
Section 49 deals with appeals, which are to the Queen's Bench Divisional Court of the High Court except for terminating a suspension or restoration to the roll, in which case they are to the MR. If, having applied to the SDT,

you wish to appeal, you may be ordered to give security for costs: RSC Order 106, rule 14.

Restoration of solicitor to the roll
The test to be applied by the SDT for restoration to the roll is: "Would any reasonably minded member of the public, knowing the facts, say `really any profession should be proud to readmit him as a member'?": 31.09.

The tribunal also takes into account the former solicitor's rehabilitation and employment history since striking off, his future intentions and whether he has reimbursed the compensation fund for any payment made by it.

Solicitors Act sections referred to: 31, 43, 46, 47 and 49.

(i) Applications to the High Court

Anyone - whether a client or not - has the right to apply to the High Court to have a solicitor struck off or to require him to answer allegations contained in an affidavit: ss. 31(2) and 51(1). The applicant must also swear an affidavit, showing that he has served the Law Society with copies of all affidavits to be relied on and given not less than 14 clear days notice: s.51(2). The Law Society may be heard in court in support of an order proposing that the solicitor be struck off or any other order proposed by the court: s.51(3). Costs may be ordered against the applicant or the solicitor or against both but not - so it seems - against the Society: s.51(4).

If the court makes an order, it should be drawn up by the applicant but, if he fails to do so within a week, it may be drawn up by the Law Society, which then becomes in effect the applicant: s.52. If the solicitor is ordered to be struck off or suspended, the court so informs the Society, which implements the order: s.53. Where an application has been made, requiring a solicitor to answer allegations, whether to the SDT or the court, it is deemed to be an application to strike off on the grounds contained in the relevant affidavit: s.55.

A more frequently used process and an extremely useful one is the right to apply under RSC Order 106, rule 3 for the delivery of a cash account, which is a schedule itemising details of all sums received and all sums expended by your solicitor, delivery up of money or securities, delivery of a list of money or securities held by your solicitor and an order for such monies or securities to be paid into court.

This application has to be made by the issue of a claim form or, if there are already proceedings relating to your application(s), in accordance with part 23 of the Civil Procedure Rules: 106, rule 3(2). If your solicitor has in effect refused to return property to you because he has not been paid, i.e. he relies on his lien, the court may make appropriate orders, including the bringing about of a detailed assessment of costs: Order 106 rules 3(3) and 5A.

The application will be heard by whoever may be the most appropriate of a costs judge or district judge of the Family Division or of a High Court District Registry. Order 106 rule 2(2). If documents have to be served on the Law Society, they should be sent to its Secretary: Order 106 rule 10. As in the case of an application to the SDT, appeals are heard by the Divisional Court of the Queens Bench: Order 106, rule 11 and security for costs may be ordered to be given by an applicant, who appeals: Order 106, rule 14. There is also power for the court, presumably on a matter of conduct, to obtain the SDT's written opinion: Order 106, rule 15.

Solicitors Act sections referred to: 31, 51, 52, 53 and 55.

Rules 2, 3, 5, 10, 11, 14 and 15 of Order 106 of the Rules of the Supreme Court, which are relevant, are set out in Appendix 3.

(j) Interventions

Interventions are directed at the solicitor's practice rather than at the solicitor personally. The consequences of an intervention, unless it is set aside, are, however, in practice as dire as striking off or suspension because on a full intervention the practice will cease to exist. The Law Society obtains possession but not ownership of the solicitor's papers and has his client and office accounts frozen.

The power to intervene: s.35 is frequently exercised for breach of the Solicitors' Accounts Rules, on bankruptcy, imprisonment, incapacity, practising uncertificated, suspension or striking off. Dishonesty is inessential. There is often a pre-requisite to notify that a power to intervene has arisen but this need not be given, if dishonesty is suspected. On intervention the OSS's Legal Services Unit will usually appoint another firm of solicitors as its agents. Unless the solicitor sells his practice, the agent will notify the solicitor's clients of the situation and invite them to find other solicitors.

An intervention can be set aside by an originating application to the Chancery Division made within eight days of the service of the notice of intervention: paragraph 6(4) Part II of Schedule 1 and RSC Order 106, rule 6.

In short, the sole solicitor or his practice will inevitably lose any good will, which will make it very difficult for him to revive his practice; he will have to start again. Even this may not be possible since an intervention automatically results in his suspension and often leads to a striking off or suspension order from the SDT.

As it would appear that only the Law Society may avail itself of the intervention procedure, it is, strictly speaking, not a remedy available to you as a client. It is, however, proposed to deal briefly with the law and practice as third persons can be affected by orders made pursuant to the powers in interventions and you, as a client, may well have initiated or be able to initiate an intervention by drawing the particular circumstances to the attention of the Law Society or the OSS.

The following is a condensed version of the circumstances justifying intervention and a simplified description of the consequences of an intervention with comments. The law as to interventions is contained in Parts I and II of Schedule 1 of the Solicitors Act, as amended.

Part I Circumstances in which Society may Intervene.

(1) Where

(a) the Council suspects dishonesty by your solicitor, his employee or, if he has died, his personal representative;

(b) the Council considers there has been undue delay by the personal representative of a sole solicitor;

(c) the Council is satisfied your solicitor has failed to comply with rules under section 32 (accounts) or section 37(2)(c) (failure to maintain insurance indemnity);

(d) your solicitor is bankrupt or has made an arrangement with his creditors;

(e) he has been imprisoned in civil or criminal proceedings;

(f) he is incapacitated by illness or accident;

(g) he has become subject to section 104 of the Mental Health Act 1959;

(h) his name has been removed or struck off or he has been suspended;

(i) he has abandoned his practice;

(j) he has become incapacitated by age;

(k) he has been subject to intervention within the previous 18 months;

(l) he has acted without a practising certificate;

(m) he is in breach of a condition on his practising certificate.

Quite clearly the circumstances covered by (a), (b), (d), (f), (i) and (j) above are quite likely to be discovered by you as a client and may well not come to the attention of the OSS unless they are made aware of them by you, some other client or another solicitor.

(2) Prior to exercising their powers under sub-paragraph (1)(c) the Society must notify the solicitor that he has failed to comply with the accounts rules or to maintain his insurance and that their powers are accordingly exercisable.

This sub-paragraph is intended to give the solicitor an opportunity to comply with his accounting and insuring obligations.

2. On the death of a sole solicitor paragraphs 6-8 apply to client accounts.

This paragraph graphically demonstrates that the purpose of an intervention is to protect your money and is not necessarily dependent on any culpability by your solicitor.

3. Powers are also exercisable where (a) there has been a complaint of undue delay in dealing with a matter, (b) the Society has invited the solicitor to give an explanation within not less than 8 days, (c) the solicitor has failed to give a satisfactory explanation and (d) the Society has notified the solicitor of his failure and that the Part II powers are exercisable.

This power of limited intervention (to obtain papers or where there has been undue delay) is exercisable by an assistant director, from whom there is a right of appeal by the solicitor to the Conduct Casework Committee.

Once again the solicitor is given an opportunity to rectify the position.

4(1) Part II powers remain exercisable after death or striking off.

(2) Paragraphs 5(1), 6(2) and (3), 8, 9(1) and (5) and 10(1) include personal representatives.

Part II - Powers Exercisable on Intervention

Money

5(1) On the Society's application, the High Court may order that no payment be made without leave of the court by any person of any money held by him for the solicitor or his firm.

(2) The order does not take effect until served and, in the case of a bank, on the appropriate branch.

(3) A person will not have disobeyed an order if he satisfies the court he exercised due diligence.

(4) This paragraph does not apply where the powers have been exercised pursuant to paragraph 3.

6(2) Where, in accordance with sub-paragraph (2),

    (a) they may exercise their powers under paragraph 1,
    (b) they may exercise their powers under paragraph 2 (sole solicitor's client accounts) and
    (c) they may exercise their powers under paragraph 3 (controlled trusts),

the Council may resolve to recover or receive the money in question provided the Society has served the solicitor and any other person having possession of the money with a certified copy of the Council's resolution and a notice prohibiting payment: (3).

(4) On receipt of a notice under sub-paragraph (3) the solicitor has 8 days, on giving not less than 48 hours written notice to the Society and its solicitors, to apply to the High Court for an order that the Society withdraws its notice.

(5) If the court makes such an order, it may also make any other order it thinks fit.

(6) If, having been notified under sub-paragraph (3), a person ignores the notice and pays out money, he is liable to summary conviction and fine on level 3 of the standard scale.

8 Without prejudice to paragraphs 5 to 7, the court may require any person reasonably suspected of holding money for the solicitor or his firm to give information as to such money and where it is held.

Documents

9(1)and (2) Where they wish to exercise their powers under paragraph 1 (general circumstances) or paragraph 3 (delay), the Society may notify the solicitor requiring him to produce or deliver at a time and place fixed by them all documents to their appointee (usually another firm of solicitors).

(3) Anyone who fails to comply with the notice to deliver shall be guilty of an offence and liable on summary conviction to a fine not exceeding level 3 unless an application has been made under (4).

(4) On the Society's application, the court may order the person, who has been so required, to produce or deliver documents to the Society's appointee.

(5) The High Court may, on the Society's application, order any person to produce and deliver documents if there is reason to suspect that such person has the documents.

Thus, by way of comment, it would appear that, in the case of a solicitor, either the Society may give notice or the court may make an order, but that as against someone other than the solicitor, only the court may make an order for production of documents.

Paragraph 9(1) seems to deal specifically with solicitors. Paragraph 9(3) seems to deal with any person failing to comply with a requirement under 9(1) and paragraph 9(4) seems also to apply to any person.

(6) The court may authorise the Law Society's appointee, (the intervener) to enter any premises by force and to search for and take possession of documents.

(7) The Society must serve notice that they have taken possession on the person from whom they took the document.

(8) The solicitor or person from whom the documents were taken by the Society may apply on 48 hours notice to the Society for an order for the documents to be delivered to the applicant's appointee.

(9) The notice under sub-paragraph (8) must be within 8 days of service of the notice under (7).

(10) The society may apply for an order to dispose of or destroy any document.

(11) On an application under (8) or (10), the court may make other orders.

(12) The Society may copy documents in its possession.

Mail

10 Except where the powers are conferred by virtue of paragraph 3, the Society may obtain an order for the redirection of the solicitor's post to itself.

Trusts

11 If the solicitor or his personal representative is a trustee of a controlled trust, the Society may obtain a court order for his substitution and he will have the same powers as if appointed under section 41 of the Trustee Act 1925.

General

12 The powers under the Schedule override any lien.

15 Any application to the Court may be heard in chambers.

Solicitors Act sections referred to: 35.

Rules 6, 7, 8 and 9 of Order 106 of the Rules of the Supreme Court, which are relevant, are set out in Appendix 3.

APPENDIX I

Solicitors Act 1974 (reproduced with the permission of the controller of Her Majesty's Stationery Office)

Section 1 - Qualifications

No person shall be qualified to act as a solicitor unless -

(a) he has been admitted as a solicitor, and

(b) his name is on the roll, and

(c) he has in force a certificate issued by the Society in accordance with the provisions of this Part authorising him to practise as a solicitor (in this Act referred to as a "practising certificate").

Section 1A - Practising certificates for employed solicitors

A person who has been admitted as a solicitor and whose name is on the roll shall, if he would not otherwise be taken to be acting as a solicitor, be taken for the purposes of this Act to be so acting if he is employed in connection with the provision of any legal services -

(a) by any person who is qualified to act as a solicitor;

(b) by any partnership at least one member of which is so qualified; or

(C) by a body recognised by the Council of the Law Society under section 9 of the Administration of Justice Act 1985 (incorporated practices).

Section 2 - Training Regulations

(1) The Society, with the concurrence of the Lord Chancellor, the Lord Chief Justice and the Master of the Rolls, may make regulations (in this Act referred to as "training regulations") about education and training for persons seeking to be admitted or to practise as solicitors.

(2) [Repealed by Courts and Legal Services Act 1990, Sched.20]

(3) Training regulations -

    (a) may prescribe -

        (i) the education and training whether by service under articles or otherwise, to be undergone by persons seeking admission as solicitors;

        (ii) any education or training to be undergone by persons who have been admitted as solicitors;

(iii) the examinations or other tests to be undergone by persons seeking admission as solicitors or who have been admitted;

(iv) the qualifications and reciprocal duties and responsibilities of persons undertaking to give education or training for the purposes of the regulations or undergoing such education or training; and

(v) the circumstances in which articles may be discharged or education or training under the regulations may be terminated;

(b) may require persons who have been admitted as solicitors to hold practising certificates while they are undergoing education or training under the regulations;

(c) may include provision for the charging of fees by the Society and the application of fees which the Society receives;

(d) may make different provision for different classes of persons and different circumstances.

(4) Where, under Schedule 4 to the Courts and Legal Services Act 1990 (approval of certain regulations in connection with the grant of rights of audience or rights to conduct litigation), the Lord Chancellor, the Lord Chief Justice or the Master of the Rolls approves any regulation made under this section he shall be taken, for the purposes of this section, to have concurred in the making of that regulation.

(5) Subsection (4) shall have effect whether or not the regulation required to be approved under Schedule 4 to the Act of 1990.

Section 13A(1) - Imposition of conditions while practising certificates are in force.

(1) Subject to the provisions of this section, the Society may in the case of any solicitor direct that his practising certificate for the time being in force (his "current certificate") shall have effect subject to such conditions as the Society may think fit.

Section 15 - Suspension of Practising Certificates

(1) The making by the Tribunal or by the court of an order suspending a solicitor from practice shall operate, and an adjudication in bankruptcy of a solicitor shall operate immediately, to suspend any practising certificate of that solicitor for the time being in force.

(1A) Where the power conferred by paragraph 6(1) or 9(1) of Schedule 1 has been exercised in relation to a solicitor by virtue of paragraph 1(1)(a)(i), (c) (so far as it applies to rules made by virtue of section 32) or (e) of that Schedule, the exercise of that power shall operate immediately to suspend any practising certificate of that solicitor for the time being in force.

(1B) Subsection (1A) does not apply if, at the time when the power referred to there is exercised, the Society directs that subsection (1A) is not to apply in relation to the solicitor concerned.

(1C) If, at the time when the power referred to in subsection (1A) is exercised, the Society gives a direction to that effect, the solicitor concerned may continue to act in relation to any matter specified in the direction as if his practising certificate had not been suspended by virtue of subsection (1A), but subject to such conditions (if any) as the Society sees fit to impose.

(2) For the purpose of this Act, a practising certificate shall be deemed not to be in force at any time while it is suspended.

Section 20 - Unqualified Person not to act

(1) No unqualified person shall -

   (a) act as a solicitor, or as such issue any writ or process, or commence, prosecute or defend any action, suit or other proceeding, in his own name or in the name of any other person, in any court of civil or criminal jurisdiction; or

   (b) act as a solicitor in any cause or matter, civil or criminal, to be heard or determined before any justice or justices or any commissioners of Her Majesty's revenue.

(2) Any person who contravenes the provision of subsection (1) -

   (a) shall be guilty of an offence and liable on conviction on indictment to imprisonment for not more than two years or to a fine or to both; and

   (b) shall be guilty of contempt of the court in which the action, suit, cause, matter or proceeding in relation to which he so acts is brought or taken and may be punished accordingly

   (c) [...]

(3) A person exempted from the provisions of section 23(1) by virtue of section 23(2) or (3) of this Act or section 55 of the Courts and Legal Services Act 1990 may, in any non-contentious or common form probate business, apply for a grant of probate or for letters of administration or oppose such an application without committing an offence under this section.

(4) In subsection (3) "non-contentious or common form probate business" has the same meaning as in section 128 of the Supreme Court Act 1981.

Section 21 - Unqualified Persons not to pretend

Any unqualified person who wilfully pretends to be, or takes or uses any name, title, addition or description implying that he is, qualified or recognised by law as qualified to act as a solicitor shall be guilty of an offence and liable on summary conviction to a fine not exceeding the fourth level on the standard scale.

Section 22 - Unqualified Persons not to prepare documents for conveyancing

(1) Subject to subsections (2) and (2A) any unqualified person who directly or indirectly -

(a) draws or prepares any instrument of transfer or charge for the purposes of the Land Registration Act 1925, or makes any application or lodges any document for registration under that Act at the registry, or

(b) draws or prepares any other instrument relating to real or personal estate, or any legal proceeding, shall, unless he proves that the act was not done for or in expectation of any fee, gain or reward, be guilty of an offence and liable on summary conviction to a fine not exceeding level 3 on the standard scale.

(2) Subsection (1) does not apply to -

   (a) a barrister or duly certified notary public;

   (aa) a registered trade mark agent drawing or preparing any instrument relating to any design, trade mark or service mark;

   (ab) a registered patent agent drawing or preparing any instrument relating to any invention, design, technical information, trade mark or service mark;

   (b) any public officer drawing or preparing instruments or applications in the course of his duty;

   (c) any person employed merely to engross any instrument, application or proceeding; and paragraph (b) of that subsection does not apply to a duly certificated solicitor in Scotland.

(2A) Subsection (1) also does not apply to any act done by a person at the direction and under the supervision of another person if -

   (a) that other person was at the time his employer, a partner of his employer or a fellow employee; and

   (b) the act could have been done by that other person for or in expectation of any fee, gain or reward without committing an offence under this section.

(3) For the purposes of subsection (1)(b) "instrument" includes a contract for the sale or other disposition of land (except a contract to grant such a lease as is referred to in section 54 (2) of the Law of Property Act 1925 (short leases)), but does not include -

   (a) a will or other testamentary instrument;

   (b) an agreement not intended to be executed as a deed other than a contract that is included by virtue of the preceding provision of this subsection;

   (c) a letter or power of attorney; or

(d) a transfer of stock containing no trust or limitation thereof.

(3A) In subsection (2) -
"registered trade mark agent" has the same meaning as in section 282(1) of the Copyright, Designs and Patents Act 1988; and "registered patent agent" has the same meaning as in section 275(1) of that Act.

(4) A local weights and measures authority may institute proceedings for an offence under this section.

Section 23 - Unqualified Persons not to prepare documents for probate

(1) Subject to subsections (2) and (3), any unqualified person, who directly or indirectly, draws or prepares any papers on which to found or oppose -

    (a) a grant of probate, or

    (b) a grant of letters of administration,

shall, unless he proves that the act was not done for or in expectation of any fee, gain or reward, be guilty of an offence and liable on summary conviction to a fine not exceeding the first level on the standard scale.

(2) Subsection (1) does not apply to -

    (a) a barrister;

    (b) a duly certificated notary public;

    (c) the Public Trustee;

    (d) the Official Solicitor;

    (e) any institution which -

        (i) is authorised by the Bank of England, under Part I of the Banking Act 1987, to carry on a deposit-taking business; and

        (ii) satisfies the conditions mentioned in subsection (2A);

    (f) any building society which -

        (i) is authorised to raise money from its members by the Building Societies Commission under section 9 of the Building Societies Act 1986; and

        (ii) satisfies these conditions;

(g) any insurance company which -

    (i) is authorised under section 3 or 4 of the Insurance Companies Act 1982; and

    (ii) satisfies those conditions;

(h) any subsidiary (as defined by section 736(1) of the Companies Act 1985) of a body falling within paragraph (e), (f) or (g) -

    (i) whose business, or any part of whose business, consists of acting as trustee or executor; and

    (ii) which satisfies those conditions.

(2A) The conditions are that the body is a member of, or otherwise subject to a scheme which -

    (a) has been established (whether or not exclusively) for the purpose of dealing with complaints about the provision of probate services; and

    (b) complies with such requirements as may be prescribed by regulations made by the Lord Chancellor with respect to matters relating to such complaints.

(3) Subsection (1) also does not apply to -

    (a) any act done by an officer or employee of a body corporate at a time when it is exempt from subsection (1) by virtue of any paragraphs (e) to (h) of subsection (2) or by virtue of section 55 of the Courts and Legal Services Act 1990 (preparation of probate papers etc); or

    (b) any act done by any person at the direction and under the supervision of another person if –

        (i) that other person was at the time his employer, a partner of his employer or a fellow employee; and

        (ii) the act could have been done by that other person for or in expectation of any fee, gain or reward without committing an offence under this section.

(4) For the avoidance of doubt, where a person does any act which would constitute an offence under subsection (1) but for an exemption given to him by this section or by or under any other enactment, he shall not be guilty of an offence under section 22 by virtue of having done that act.

Section 25 - Costs where unqualified person acts

(1) No costs in respect of anything done by any unqualified person acting as a solicitor shall be recoverable by him, or by any other person, in any action, suit or matter.

(2) Nothing in subsection (1) shall prevent the recovery of money paid or to be paid by a solicitor while acting for the client without holding a practising certificate in force if that money would have been recoverable if he had held such a certificate when so acting.

(3) For the avoidance of doubt, where a person does an act which would be an offence under section 23 were it not for the provisions of section 54 or 55 of the Courts and Legal Services Act 1990, this section does not apply in relation to that act.

Section 28 - Regulations

(1) The Master of the Rolls may make regulations, with the concurrence of the Lord Chancellor and the Lord Chief Justice, about the following matters, namely -

    (a) admission as a solicitor;

    (b) the keeping of the roll;

    (c) practising certificates and applications for them;

    (d) the keeping of the register under section 9.

(2) The power conferred by subsection (1) includes power to specify -

    (a) one or more conditions (in this Act referred to as "training conditions") to be imposed on the issue of practising certificates to solicitors to whom training regulations apply; and

    (b) one or more conditions (in this Act referred to as "indemnity conditions") to be imposed on the issue of practising certificates to solicitors who are exempt from indemnity rules.

(3) Regulations about the keeping of the roll and of the register under section 9 may provide for the manner in which entries are to be made, altered and removed.

(3A) Regulations about the keeping of the roll may -

    (a) provide for the Society, at such intervals as may be specified in the regulations, to enquire of solicitors of any class so specified whether they wish to have their names retained on the roll;

    (b) require solicitors of any such class, at such intervals as aforesaid, to pay to the Society a fee in respect of the retention of their names on the roll of such amount as may be prescribed by the regulations; and

    (c) authorise the Society to remove from the roll the name of any solicitor who -

        (i) fails to reply to any enquiry made in pursuance of paragraph (a) or to pay any fee payable by virtue of paragraph (b) or

(ii) replies to any such enquiry by indicating that he does not wish to have his name retained on the roll;

(d) authorise the Society to remove from the roll the name of any solicitor who has died.

(4) Regulations about the keeping of the roll may also provide for rights of appeal to the Master of the Rolls in connection with the making and alteration of entries on the roll and the removal of entries from it.

(5) The Master of the Rolls may make regulations about the procedure for any appeals to him authorised by this Part or regulations under this section.

Section 31 - Rules as to professional practice, conduct and discipline

Without prejudice to any other provision of this Part the Council may, if they think fit, make rules, with the concurrence of the Master of the Rolls, for regulating in respect of any matter the professional practice, conduct and discipline of solicitors.

(2) If any solicitor fails to comply with rules made under this section, any person may make a complaint in respect of that failure to the Tribunal.

{(3) and (4) not here reproduced}

Section 32 - Accounts Rules

(1) The Council shall make rules, with the concurrence of the Master of the Rolls -

(a) as to the opening and keeping by solicitors of accounts at banks or with building societies for clients' money; and

(b) as to the keeping by solicitors of accounts containing particulars and information as to money received or held or paid by them for or on account of their clients; and

(c) empowering the Council to take such action as may be necessary to enable them to ascertain whether or not the rules are being complied with;

and the rules may specify the location of the banks' branches at which the accounts are to be kept.

(2) The Council shall also make rules, with the concurrence of the Master of the Rolls -

(a) as to the opening and keeping by solicitors of accounts at banks or with building societies for money comprised in controlled trusts; and

(b) as to the keeping by solicitors of accounts containing particulars and information as to money received or held or paid by them for or on account of any such trust; and

(c) empowering the Council to take such action as may be necessary to enable them to ascertain whether or not the rules are being complied with.

and the rules may specify the location of the banks' branches at which the accounts are to be kept.

(3) If any solicitor fails to comply with rules made under this section, any person may make a complaint in respect of that failure to the Tribunal.

(4) The Council shall be at liberty to disclose a report on or information about a solicitor's accounts obtained in the exercise of powers conferred by rules made under subsection (1) or (2) to the Director of Public Prosecutions for use in investigating the possible commission of an offence by the solicitor and, if the Director thinks fit, for use in connection with any prosecution of the solicitor consequent on the investigation.

(5) Rules under this section may specify circumstances in which solicitors or any class of solicitors are exempt from the rules by virtue of their office or employment.

(6) For the purposes of this section and section 33 references to clients' money and money of a kind mentioned in subsection (1)(b) of this section or (1)(a) of section 33 include references to money held by a solicitor as a stakeholder (whether or not paid by a client of his).

Section 33 - Interest on client's money

(1) Rules made under section 32 shall make provision for requiring a solicitor, in such cases as may be prescribed by the rules, either -

    (a) to keep on deposit in a separate account at a bank or with a building society for the benefit of the client money received for or on account of a client; or

    (b) to make good to the client out of the solicitor's own money a sum equivalent to the interest which would have accrued if the money so received had been so kept on deposit.

(2) The cases in which a solicitor may be required by the rules to act as mentioned in subsection (1) may be defined, among other things, by reference to the amount of any sum received or the period for which it is or is likely to be retained or both; and the rules may include provision for enabling a client (without prejudice to any other remedy) to require that any question arising under the rules in relation to the client's money be referred to and determined by the Society.

(3) Except as provided by the rules, a solicitor shall not be liable by virtue of the relation between solicitor and client to account to any client for interest received by the solicitor on money deposited at a bank or with a building society being money received or held for or on account of his clients generally.

(4) Nothing in this section or in the rules shall -

    (a) affect any arrangement in writing, whenever made, between a solicitor and his client as to the application of the client's money or interest on it;

    (b) ...

APPENDIX 1

Section 34 - Accountants' Reports

(1) Every solicitor shall once in each period of twelve months ending with 31st October, unless the Council are satisfied that it is unnecessary for him to do so deliver to the Society, whether by post or otherwise, a report signed by an accountant (in this section referred to as an "accountant's report") and containing such information as may be prescribed by rules made by the Council under this section.

(2) An accountant's report shall be delivered to the Society not more than six months (or such other period as may be prescribed by rules made under this section) after the end of the accounting period for the purposes of that report.

(3) Subject to any rules made under this section, the accounting period for the purposes of an accountant's report -

    (a) shall begin at the expiry of the last preceding accounting period for which an accountant's report has been delivered;

    (b) shall cover not less than twelve months; and

    (c) where possible, consistently with the preceding provision of this section, shall correspond to a period or consecutive periods for which the accounts of the solicitor or his firm are ordinarily made up.

(4) The Council shall make rules to give effect to the provisions of this section, and those rules shall prescribe -

    (a) the qualification to be held by an accountant by whom an accountant's report is given;

    (b) the information to be contained in an accountant's report.

    (c) the nature and extent of the examination to be made by an accountant of the books and accounts of a solicitor or his firm and of any other relevant documents with a view to the signing of an accountant's report;

    (d) the form of an accountant's report; and

    (e) the evidence, if any, which shall satisfy the Council that the delivery of an accountant's report is unnecessary and the cases in which such evidence is or is not required.

(5) Rules under this section may include provision -

    (a) permitting in such special circumstances as may be defined by the rules a different accounting period from that specified in subsection (3); and

    (b) regulating any matters of procedure or matters incidental, ancillary or supplemental to the provisions of this section.

(5A) Without prejudice to the generality of subsection (5) (b), rules under this section may make provision requiring a solicitor in advance of delivering an accountant's report to notify the Society of the period which is to be the accounting period for the purposes of that report in accordance with the preceding provisions of this section.

(6) If any solicitor fails to comply with the provisions of this section or of any rules made under it, a complaint in respect of that failure may be made to the Tribunal by or on behalf of the Society.

(7) A certificate under the hand of the Secretary of the Society shall, until the contrary is proved, be evidence that a solicitor has or, as the case may be, has not delivered to the Society an accountant's report or supplied evidence required under this section or any rules made under it.

(8) Where a solicitor is exempt from rules under section 32 -

    (a) nothing in this section shall apply to him unless he takes out a practising certificate;

    (b) an accountant's report shall in no case deal with books, accounts or documents kept by him in the course of employment by virtue of which he is exempt from those rules; and

    (c) no examination shall be made of any such books, accounts and documents under any rules made under this section.

Section 35 - Intervention under Schedule 1

The powers conferred by Part II of Schedule 1 shall be exercisable in the circumstances specified in Part I of that Schedule.

Section 36 - Compensation Fund under Schedule 2

(1) The fund, known as the "Compensation Fund" shall be maintained and administered in accordance with the provisions of Schedule 2.

(2) Where the Council are satisfied -

    (a) that a person has suffered or is likely to suffer loss in consequence of dishonesty on the part of a solicitor, or of an employee of a solicitor, in connection with that solicitor's practice or purported practice or in connection with any trust of which that solicitor is or formerly was a trustee; or

    (b) that a person has suffered or is likely to suffer hardship in consequence of failure on the part of a solicitor to account for money which has come to his hands in connection with his practice or purported practice or in connection with any trust of which he is or formerly was a trustee; or

APPENDIX 1

    (c) that a solicitor has suffered or is likely to suffer loss or hardship by reason of his liability to any of his or his firm's clients in consequence of some act or default of any of his partners or employees in circumstances where but for the liability of that solicitor a grant might have been made out of the Compensation Fund to some other person;

the Society may make a grant out of the Compensation Fund for the purpose of relieving that loss or hardship.

(3) A grant under subsection (2) (c) may be made by way of a loan upon such terms and conditions including terms and conditions as to the time and manner of repayment, the payment of interest and the giving of security for repayment (as the Council may determine, and the Society may at any time or times, upon such terms and conditions if any) as the Council think fit, waive or refrain from enforcing the repayment of the whole or any part of the loan, the payment of any interest on the loan or any of its terms and conditions.

(4) Where -

    (a) a grant is made otherwise than by way of loan, or

    (b) a grant is made by way of loan and a condition specified in subsection (5) is satisfied in relation to it,

the Society shall be subrogated, to the extent specified in subsection (6) to any rights and remedies of the person to whom the grant is made in relation to the act or default in respect of which it is made, and shall be entitled, upon giving him a sufficient indemnity against costs, to require him, whether before or after payment of the grant, to sue in his own name but on behalf o the Society for the purpose of giving effect to the Society's rights, and to permit the Society to have the conduct of the proceedings.

(5) The conditions mentioned in subsection (4) are -

    (a) that repayment of the whole or part of the loan has been waived;

    (b) that the borrower has failed to repay the whole or part of the loan in accordance with the terms and conditions of the loan.

(6) The extent to which the Society is subrogated under subsection (4) is -

    (a) for a grant made by way of loan, the amount in relation to which a condition specified in subsection (5) is satisfied, and

    (b) for any other grant, the amount of the grant.

(7) Where the Society refuses a grant, the Council shall state the reasons for the refusal.

(8) The Council may make rules about the Compensation Fund and the procedure for making grants from it.

A STRAIGHTFORWARD GUIDE TO YOU AND YOUR SOLICITOR

Section 37 - Professional Indemnity

(1) The Council, with the concurrence of the Master of the Rolls, may make rules (in this Act referred to as "indemnity rules") concerning indemnity against loss arising from claims in respect of any description of civil liability incurred -

   (a) by a solicitor or a former solicitor in connection with his practice or with any trust of which he is or formerly was a trustee;

   (b) by an employee or former employee of a solicitor or former solicitor in connection with that solicitor's practice or with any trust of which that solicitor or the employee is or formerly was a trustee.

(2) For the purpose of providing such indemnity, indemnity rules -

   (a) may authorise or require the Society to establish and maintain a fund or funds;

   (b) may authorise or require the Society to take out and maintain insurance with authorised insurers;

   (c) may require solicitors or any specified class of solicitors to take out and maintain insurance with authorised insurers.

(3) Without prejudice to the generality of subsections (1) and (2) indemnity rules -

   (a) may specify the terms and conditions on which indemnity is to be available, and any circumstances in which the right is to be excluded or modified;

   (b) may provide for the management, administration and protection of any fund maintained by virtue of subsection (2) (a) and require solicitors or any class of solicitors to make payments to any such fund;

   (c) may require solicitors or any class of solicitors to make payments by way of premium on any insurance policy maintained by the Society by virtue of subsection (2) (b);

   (d) may prescribe the conditions which an insurance policy must satisfy for the purposes of subsection (2) (c);

   (e) may authorise the Society to determine the amount of any payments required by the rules, subject to such limits, or in accordance with such provisions, as may be prescribed by the rules;

   (f) may specify circumstances in which, where a solicitor for whom indemnity is provided has failed to comply with the rules, the Society or insurers may take proceedings against him in respect of sums paid by way of indemnity in connection with a matter in relation to which he has failed to comply;

APPENDIX 1

    (g)   may specify circumstances in which solicitors are exempt from the rules;

    (h)   may empower the Council to take such steps as they consider necessary or expedient to ascertain whether or not the rules are being complied with; and

    (i)   may contain incidental, procedural or supplementary provisions.

(4) If any solicitor fails to comply with indemnity rules, any person may make a complaint in respect of that failure to the Tribunal.

(5) The Society shall have power, without prejudice to any of its other powers, to carry into effect any arrangements which it considers necessary or expedient for the purpose of indemnity under this section.

Section 37A - Redress for inadequate professional services

Schedule 1A shall have effect with respect to the provision by solicitors of services which are not of the quality which it is reasonable to expect of them.

Section 43 - Control of employment of certain clerks

(1) Where a person who is or was a clerk to a solicitor but is not himself a solicitor -

    (a)   has been convicted of a criminal offence which discloses such dishonesty that in the opinion of the Society it would be undesirable for him to be employed by a solicitor in connection with his practice; or

    (b)   has, in the opinion of the Society, occasioned or been a party to, with or without the connivance of the solicitor to whom he is or was clerk, an act or default in relation to that solicitor's practice which involved conduct on his part of such a nature that in the opinion of the Society it would be undesirable for him to be employed by a solicitor in connection with his practice,

an application may be made to the Tribunal with respect to that person by or on behalf of the Society.

(2) The Tribunal, on the hearing of any application under subsection (1) may make an order that as from such date as may be specified in the order no solicitor shall, except in accordance with permission in writing granted by the Society for such period and subject to such conditions as the Society may think fit to specify in the permission, employ or remunerate, in connection with his practice as a solicitor, the person with respect to whom the application is made.

(3) An order made by the Tribunal under subsection (2) may, on the application of the Society or of the person with respect to whom the application for the order was made, be revoked by a subsequent order of the Tribunal; and where in the opinion of the Tribunal no prima facie case is shown in favour of an application for revocation, the Tribunal may refuse the application without hearing the applicant.

(4) The Tribunal, on the hearing of any application under this section, may make an order as to the payment of costs by any party to the application.

(5) Orders made under this section and filed with the Society may be inspected by any solicitor during office hours without payment but shall not be open to the inspection of any person other than a solicitor.

(6) [...]

(7) For the purposes of this section an order under Part I of the Powers of Criminal Courts Act 1973, discharging a person absolutely or conditionally shall, notwithstanding anything in section 1C of that Act, be deemed to be a conviction of the offence for which the order was made.

Section 44B - Power of Society to examine files in connection with complaints

(1) Where the Council are satisfied that it is necessary to do so for the purpose of investigating any complaint made to the Society -

    (a) alleging professional misconduct by a solicitor; or

    (b) relating to the quality of any professional services provided by a solicitor,

the Society may give notice to the solicitor or his firm requiring the production or delivery to any person appointed by the Society, at a time and place to be fixed by the Society, of all documents in the possession of the solicitor or his firm in connection with the matters to which the complaint relates (whether or not they relate also to other matters).

(2) Sub-paragraphs (2) to (12) of paragraphs 9 of Schedule 1, together with paragraphs 12 to 16 of that Schedule, shall apply in relation to the powers conferred by subsection (1) as they apply in relation to the powers conferred by sub-paragraph (1) of paragraph 9, and accordingly in those provisions -

    (a) any reference to a person appointed, or to a requirement, under that sub-paragraph shall be construed as including a reference to a person appointed, or to a requirement, under subsection (1); and

    (b) any reference to any such documents as are mentioned in that sub-paragraph shall be construed as including a reference to any such documents as are mentioned in subsection (1).

Section 46 - Solicitors Disciplinary Tribunal

(1) Applications and complaints made by virtue of any provision of this Act shall be made, except so far as other provision is made by this Act or by any regulations under it, to the tribunal known as the "Solicitors Disciplinary Tribunal".

(2) The Master of the Rolls shall appoint the members of the Tribunal.

(3) The Tribunal shall consist -

APPENDIX 1

    (a)   of practising solicitors of not less than ten years' standing (in this section referred to as "solicitor members"); and

    (b)   of persons who are neither solicitors nor barristers (in this section referred to as "lay members").

(4)   A member of the Tribunal shall hold and vacate his office in accordance with the terms of his appointment and shall, on ceasing to hold office, be eligible for re-appointment.

(5)   There shall be paid to the lay members out of money provided by Parliament such fees and allowances as the Lord Chancellor may, with the approval of the Minister for the Civil Service, determine.

(6)   Subject to subsections (7) and (8) the Tribunal shall be deemed to be properly constituted if -

    (a)   at least three members are present; and

    (b)   at least one lay member is present; and

    (c)   the number of solicitor members present exceeds the number of lay members present.

(7)   For the purposes of hearing and determining applications and complaints the Tribunal shall consist of not more than three members.

(8)   A decision of the Tribunal on an application or complaint may be announced by a single member.

(9)   Subject to subsections (6) to (8) the Tribunal, with the concurrence of the Master of the Rolls, may make rules -

    (a)   empowering the Tribunal to elect a solicitor member to be its president; and

    (b)   about the procedure and practice to be followed in relation to the making, hearing and determination of applications and complaints.

(10)   Without prejudice to the generality of subsection (9) (b) rules made by virtue of that paragraph may in particular -

    (a)   empower the president of the Tribunal to appoint a chairman for the hearing and determination of any application or complaint;

    (b)   provide that, if the president does not appoint a chairman, a solicitor member shall act as chairman; and

    (c)   provide, in relation to any application or complaint relating to a solicitor, that, where in the opinion of the Tribunal no prima facie case in favour of the applicant or complainant is shown in the application or complaint, the Tribunal may make an order refusing the

A STRAIGHTFORWARD GUIDE TO YOU AND YOUR SOLICITOR

application or dismissing the complaint without requiring the solicitor to whom it relates to answer the allegations and without hearing the applicant or complainant.

(11) For the purposes of any application or complaint made to the Tribunal under this Act, the Tribunal may administer oaths, and the applicant or complainant and any person with respect to whom the application or complaint is made (or, in the case of an application under section 47(1)(b) any of the parties to the application) may issue writs or subpoena ad testificandum and duces tecum, but no person shall be compelled under any such writ to produce any document which he could not be compelled to produce on the trial of an action.

(12) The power to make rules conferred by subsection (9) shall be exercisable by statutory instrument, and the Statutory Instruments Act 1946 shall apply to a statutory instrument containing such rules in like manner as if the rules had been made by a Minister of the Crown.

Section 47 - Jurisdiction and Powers of SDT

(1) Any application -

- (a) to strike the name of a solicitor off the roll;

- (b) to require a solicitor to answer allegations contained in an affidavit;

- (c) to require a former solicitor whose name has been removed from or struck off the roll to answer allegations contained in an affidavit relating to a time when he was a solicitor;

- (d) by a solicitor who has been suspended from practice for an unspecified period, by order of the Tribunal, for the termination of that suspension;

- (e) ...

- (f) ...

shall be made to the Tribunal; but nothing in this section shall affect any jurisdiction over solicitors exercisable by the Master of the Rolls, or by any judge of the High Court, by virtue of section 50.

(2)... on the hearing of any application or complaint made to the Tribunal under this Act... section 43, the Tribunal shall have power to make such order as it may think fit, and any such order may in particular include provision for any of the following matters -

- (a) the striking off the roll of the name of the solicitor to whom the application or complaint relates;

- (b) the suspension of that solicitor from practice indefinitely or for a specified period;

- (c) the payment by that solicitor or former solicitor of a penalty not exceeding £5,000, which shall be forfeit to Her Majesty;

APPENDIX 1

(d) in the circumstances referred to in subsection (2A), the exclusion of that solicitor from legal aid work (either permanently or for a specified period).

{(e) to (I) not here reproduced}

Section 49 - Appeals from Tribunal

(1) An appeal from the Tribunal shall lie -

(a) in the case of an order on an application under section 43(3) or 47(1)(d), (e) or (f) or the refusal of any such application, to the Master of the Rolls;

(b) in any other case, to the High Court.

(2) Subject to subsection (3) an appeal shall lie at the instance of the applicant or complainant or of the person with respect to whom the application or complaint was made.

(3) An appeal against an order under section 43(2) shall lie only at the instance of the person with respect to whom the application was made [and an appeal against an order under section 47 excluding any person or persons from legal aid work (within the meaning of that section) shall lie only at the instance of any person so excluded.]

(4) The High Court and the Master of the Rolls shall have power to make such order on an appeal under this section as they may think fit.

(5) Subject to any rules of court, on an appeal against an order made by virtue of rules under section 46(10)(c) without hearing the applicant or complainant, the court -

(a) shall not be obliged to hear the appellant, and

(b) may remit the matter to the Tribunal instead of dismissing the appeal.

(6) Any decision of the Master of the Rolls on an appeal under this section and any decision of the High Court on an appeal against an order under section 43(2) shall be final.

(7) The Master of the Rolls may make regulations about appeals to him under this section.

Section 51 - Procedure upon certain application to High Court

(1) Where an application to strike the name of a solicitor off the roll or to require a solicitor to answer allegations contained in an affidavit is made to the High Court, then, subject to section 54, the following provisions of this section shall have effect in relation to that application.

(2) The court shall not entertain the application except on production of an affidavit proving that the applicant has served on the Society fourteen clear days' notice of his intention to make the application,

together with copies of all affidavits intended to be used in support of the application.

(3) The Society may appear by counsel on the hearing of the application and any other proceedings arising out of or in reference to the application, and may apply to the court -

    (a) to make absolute any order nisi which the court may have made on the application;

    (b) to make an order that the name of the solicitor be struck off the roll; or

    (c) to make such other order as the court may think fit.

(4) The Court may order the costs of the Society of or relating to any of the matters mentioned in subsections (2) and (3) to be paid by the solicitor against whom, or by the person by whom, the application was made, or was intended to be made, or partly by one and partly by the other of them.

Section 52 - Drawing up Order

Where an order, whether nisi or absolute, is made by the High Court or the Court of Appeal on a motion to strike the name of a solicitor off the roll, or to require a solicitor to answer allegations contained in an affidavit, and that order is not drawn up by the applicant within one week of its being made, the Society may cause the order to be drawn up, and all future proceedings on the order shall be taken as if the motion had been made by the Society.

Section 53 - Production of Order

Where an order is made by the High Court or the Court of Appeal that the name of a solicitor be struck off the roll, or that a solicitor be suspended from practice, the proper officer of the court shall forthwith send a copy of the order to the Society, and the Society shall enter a note of the order on the roll against the name of the solicitor and, where the order so directs, shall strike that name off the roll.

Section 55 - Application requiring Solicitor to answer affidavit allegations

For the avoidance of doubt it is hereby declared that an application by any person to require a solicitor to answer allegations contained in an affidavit, whether that application is made to the Tribunal or to the High Court, may be treated as an application to strike the name of that solicitor off the roll on the grounds of the matters alleged.

Section 56 - Orders as to remuneration for non-contentious business

(1) For the purposes of this section there shall be a committee consisting of the following persons -

    (a) the Lord Chancellor;

    (b) the Lord Chief Justice;

    (c) the Master of the Rolls;

APPENDIX 1

    (d)   the President of the Society;

    (e)   a solicitor, being the president of a local law society, nominated by the Lord Chancellor to serve on the committee during his tenure of office as president; and

    (f)   for the purpose only of prescribing and regulating the remuneration of solicitors in respect of business done under the Land Registration Act 1925, the Chief Land Registrar appointed under that Act.

(2)   The committee, or any three members of the committee (the Lord Chancellor being one) may make general orders prescribing and regulating in such manner as they think fit the remuneration of solicitors in respect of non-contentious business.

(3)   The Lord Chancellor, before any order under this section is made, shall cause a draft of the order to be sent to the Council: and the committee shall consider any observations of the Council submitted to them in writing within one month of the sending of the draft, and may then make the order, either in the form of the draft or with such alterations or additions as they may think fit.

(4)   An order under this section may prescribe the mode of remuneration of solicitors in respect of non-contentious business by providing that they shall be remunerated -

    (a)   according to a scale of rates of commission or a scale of percentages, varying or not in different classes of business; or

    (b)   by a gross sum; or

    (c)   by a fixed sum for each document prepared or perused, without regard to length; or

    (d)   in any other mode; or

    (e)   partly in one mode and partly in another.

(5)   An order under this section may regulate the amount of such remuneration with reference to all or any of the following, among other, considerations, that is to say -

    (a)   the position of the party for whom the solicitor is concerned in the business, that is, whether he is vendor or purchaser, lessor or lessee, mortgagor or mortgagee, or the like;

    (b)   the place where, and the circumstances in which, the business or any part of it is transacted;

    (c)   the amount of the capital money or rent to which the business relates;

    (d)   the skill, labour and responsibility on the part of the solicitor which the business involves;

    (e)   the number and importance of the documents prepared or perused without regard to length.

(6) An order under this section may authorise and regulate -

    (a) the taking by a solicitor from his client as security for payment of any remuneration, to be ascertained by taxation or otherwise, which may become due to him under any such order; and

    (b) the allowance of interest.

(7) So long as an order made under this section is in operation the taxation of bills of costs of solicitors in respect of non-contentious business shall, subject to the provisions of section 57, be regulated by that order.

(8) Any order made under this section may be varied or revoked by a subsequent order so made.

(9) The power to make orders under this section shall be exercisable by statutory instrument which shall be subject to annulment in pursuance of a resolution of either House of Parliament; and the Statutory Instruments Act 1946 shall apply to a statutory instrument containing such an order in like manner as if the order had been made by a Minister of the Crown.

Section 57 - Non-contentious business agreements

(1) Whether or not any order is in force under section 56, a solicitor and his client may, before or after or in the course of the transaction of any non-contentious business by the solicitor, make an agreement as to his remuneration in respect of that business.

(2) The agreement may provide for the remuneration of the solicitor by a gross sum, or by reference to an hourly rate, or by a commission or percentage, or by a salary, or otherwise, and it may be made on the terms that the amount of the remuneration stipulated for shall or shall not include all or any disbursements made by the solicitor in respect of searches, plans, travelling, stamps, fees or other matters.

(3) The agreement shall be in writing and signed by the person to be bound by it or his agent in that behalf.

(4) Subject to subsections (5) and (7) the agreement may be sued and recovered on or set aside in the like manner and on the like grounds as an agreement not relating to the remuneration of a solicitor.

(5) If on any taxation of costs the agreement is relied on by the solicitor and objected to by the client as unfair or unreasonable, the taxing officer may enquire into the facts and certify them to the court, and if from that certificate it appears just to the court that the agreement should be set aside, or the amount payable under it reduced, the court may so order and may give such consequential directions as it thinks fit.

(6) Subsection (7) applies where the agreement provides for the remuneration of the solicitors to be by reference to an hourly rate.

(7) If, on the taxation of any costs, the agreement is relied on by the solicitor and the client objects to the amount of the costs (but is not alleging that the agreement is unfair or unreasonable), the taxing officer

APPENDIX 1

may enquire into -

    (a)   the number of hours worked by the solicitor; and

    (b)   whether the number of hours worked by him was excessive.

Section 58 - Remuneration of a solicitor who is mortgagee

(1)   Where a mortgage is made to a solicitor, either alone or jointly with any other person, he or the firm Of which he is a member shall be entitled to recover from the mortgagor in respect of all business transacted and acts done by him or them in negotiating the loan, deducing and investigating the title to the property, and preparing and completing the mortgage, such usual costs as he or they would have been entitled to receive if the mortgage had been made to a person who was not a solicitor and that person had retained and employed him or them to transact that business and do those acts.

(2)   Where a mortgage has been made to, or has become vested by transfer or transmission in, a solicitor, either alone or jointly with any other person, and any business is transacted or acts are done by that solicitor or by the firm of which he is a member in relation to that mortgage or the security thereby created or the property thereby charged, he or they shall be entitled to recover from the person on whose behalf the business was transacted or the acts were done, and to charge against the security, such usual costs as he or they would have been entitled to receive if the mortgage had been made and had remained vested in a person who was not a solicitor and that person had retained and employed him or them to transact that business and do so those acts.

(3)   In this section "mortgage" includes any charge on any property for securing money or money's worth.

Section 59 - Contentious business agreements

(1)   Subject to subsection (2) a solicitor may make an agreement in writing with his client as to his remuneration in respect of any contentious business done, or to be done, by him (in this Act referred to as a "contentious business agreement") providing that he shall be remunerated by a gross sum, or by reference to any hourly rate, or by a salary, or otherwise and whether at a higher or lower rate than that at which he would otherwise have been entitled to be remunerated.

(2)   Nothing in this section or in section 60 to 63 shall give validity to -

    (a)   any purchase by a solicitor of the interest, or any part of the interest, of his client in any action, suit or other contentious proceeding; or

    (b)   any agreement by which a solicitor retained or employed to prosecute any action, suit or other contentious proceeding, stipulates for payment only in the event of success in that action, suit or proceeding; or

    (c)   any disposition, contract, settlement, conveyance, delivery, dealing or transfer which under the law relating to bankruptcy is invalid against a trustee or creditor in any bankruptcy or composition.

Section 60 - Effect of contentious business agreements

(1) Subject to the provisions of this section and to sections 61 to 63, the costs of a solicitor in any case where a contentious business agreement has been made shall not be subject to taxation or (except in the case of an agreement which provides for the solicitor to be remunerated by reference to an hourly rate) to the provisions of section 69.

(2) Subject to subsection (3) a contentious business agreement shall not affect the amount of, or any rights or remedies for the recovery of, any costs payable by the client to, or to the client by, any person other than the solicitor and that person may, unless he has otherwise agreed, require any such costs to be taxed according to the rules for their taxation for the time being in force.

(3) A client shall not be entitled to recover from any other person under an order for the payment of any costs to which a contentious business agreement relates more than the amount payable by him to his solicitor in respect of those costs under the agreement.

(4) A contentious business agreement shall be deemed to exclude any claim by the solicitor in respect of the business to which it relates other than -

    (a) a claim for the agreed costs; or

    (b) a claim for such costs as are expressly excepted from the agreement.

(5) A provision in a contentious business agreement that the solicitor shall not be liable for negligence, or that he shall be relieved from any responsibility to which he would otherwise be subject as a solicitor, shall be void.

Section 61 - Enforcement of contentious business agreements

(1) No action shall be brought on any contentious business agreement, but on the application of any person who -

    (a) is a party to the agreement or the representative of such a party; or

    (b) is or is alleged to be liable to pay, or is or claims to be entitled to be paid, the costs due or alleged to be due in respect of the business to which the agreement relates,

the court may enforce or set aside the agreement and determine every question as to its validity or effect.

(2) On any application under subsection (1) the court -

    (a) if it is of the opinion that the agreement is in all respects fair and reasonable, may enforce it;

APPENDIX 1

(b) if it is of the opinion that the agreement is in any respect unfair or unreasonable, may set it aside and order the costs covered by it to be taxed as if it had never been made;

(c) in any case, may make such order as to the costs of the application as it thinks fit.

(2) If the business covered by a contentious business agreement (not being an agreement to which section 62 applies) is business done, or to be done, in any action, a client who is a party to the agreement may make application to a taxing officer of the court for the agreement to be examined.

(3) A taxing officer before whom an agreement is laid under subsection (3) shall examine it and may either allow it, or, if he is of the opinion that the agreement is unfair or unreasonable, require the opinion of the court to be taken on it, and the court may allow the agreement or reduce the amount payable under it, or set it aside and order the costs covered by it to be taxed as if it had never been made.

(4A) Subsection (4B) applies where a contentious business agreement provides for the remuneration of the solicitor to be by reference to an hourly rate.

(4B) If on the taxation of any costs the agreement is relied on by the solicitor and the client objects to the amount of the costs (but is not alleging that the agreement is unfair or unreasonable), the taxing officer may enquire into -

(a) the number of hours worked by the solicitor; and

(b) whether the number of hours worked by him was excessive.

(5) Where the amount agreed under any contentious business agreement is paid by or on behalf of the client or by any person entitled to do so, the person making the payment may at any time within twelve months from the date of payment, or within such further time as appears to the courts to be reasonable, apply to the court, and if it appears to the court that the special circumstances of the case require it to be re-opened, the court may, on such terms as may be just, re-open it and order the costs covered by the agreement to be taxed and the whole or any part of the amount received by the solicitor to be repaid by him.

(6) In this section and in sections 62 and 63 "the court" means -

(a) in relation to an agreement under which any business has been done in any court having jurisdiction to enforce and set aside agreements, any such court in which any of that business has been done;

(b) in relation to an agreement under which no business has been done in any such court and under which more than £50 is payable, the High Court;

(c) in relation to an agreement under which no business has been done in any such court and under which not more than £50 is payable, any county court which would, but for the provisions of subsection (1) prohibiting the bringing of an action on the agreement, have had jurisdiction in any action on it;

and for the avoidance of doubt it is hereby declared that in paragraph (a) "court having jurisdiction to enforce and set aside agreements" includes a county court.

Section 62 - Contentious business agreements by certain representatives

(1) Where the client who makes a contentious business agreement makes it as a representative of a person whose property will be chargeable with the whole or part of the amount payable under the agreement, the agreement, that agreement shall be laid before a taxing officer of the court before payment.

(2) A taxing officer before whom an agreement is laid under subsection (1) shall examine it and may either allow it, or, if he is of the opinion that it is unfair or unreasonable, require the opinion of the court to be taken on it, and the court may allow the agreement or reduce the amount payable under it, or set it aside and order the costs covered by it to be taxed as if it had never been made.

(3) A client who makes a contentious business agreement as mentioned in subsection (1) and pays the whole or any part of the amount payable under the agreement without it being allowed by the officer or by the court shall be liable at any time to account to the person whose property is charged with the whole or any part of the amount so paid for the sum so charged, and the solicitor who accepts the payment may be ordered by the court to refund the amount received by him.

(4) A client makes a contentious business agreement as the representative of another person if he makes it -

    (a) as his guardian,

    (b) as a trustee for him under a deed or will,

    (c) as his receiver appointed under Part VII of the Mental Health Act 1983, or

    (d) as a person other than a receiver authorised under that Part of that Act to act on his behalf.

Section 63 - Effect on contentious business agreement of death, incapability or change of solicitor.

(1) If, after some business has been done under a contentious business agreement but before the solicitor has wholly performed it -

    (a) the solicitor dies, or becomes incapable of acting; or

    (b) the client changes his solicitor (as, notwithstanding the agreement, he shall be entitled to do)

any party to, or the representative of any party to, the agreement may apply to the court, and the court shall have the same jurisdiction as to enforcing the agreement so far as it has been performed, or setting it aside, as the court would have had if the solicitor had not died or become incapable of acting, or the client had not changed his solicitor.

APPENDIX 1

(2) The court, notwithstanding that it is of the opinion that the agreement is in all respects fair and reasonable, may order the amount due in respect of business under the agreement to be ascertained by taxation, and in that case -

   (a) the taxing officer, in ascertaining that amount, shall have regard so far as may be to the terms of the agreement; and

   (b) payment of the amount found by him to be due may be enforced in the same manner as if the agreement had been completely performed.

(3) If in such a case as is mentioned in subsection (1)(b) an order is made for the taxation of the amount due to the solicitor in respect of the business done under the agreement, the court shall direct the taxing officer to have regard to the circumstances under which the change of solicitor has taken place, and the taxing officer, unless he is of the opinion that there has been no default, negligence, improper delay or other conduct on the part of the solicitor affording the client reasonable ground for changing his solicitor, shall not allow to the solicitor the full amount of the remuneration agreed to be paid to him.

Section 64 - Form of bill of costs for contentious business

(1) Where the remuneration of a solicitor in respect of contentious business done by him is not the subject of a contentious business agreement, then, subject to subsections (2) to (4) the solicitor's bill of costs may at the option of the solicitor be either a bill containing detailed items or a gross sum bill.

(2) The party chargeable with a gross sum bill may at any time -

   (a) before he is served with a writ or other originating process for the recovery of costs included in the bill, and

   (b) before the expiration of three months from the date on which the bill was delivered to him, require the solicitor to deliver, in lieu of that bill, a bill containing detailed items; and on such a requirement being made the gross sum bill shall be of no effect.

(3) Where an action is commenced on a gross sum bill, the court shall, if so requested by the party chargeable with the bill before the expiration of one month from the service on that party of the writ or other originating process, order that the bill be taxed.

(4) If a gross sum bill is taxed, whether under this section or otherwise, nothing in this section shall prejudice any rules of court with respect to taxation, and the solicitor shall furnish the taxing officer with such details of any of the costs covered by the bill as the taxing officer may require.

Section 65 - Security for costs and termination of retainer

(1) A solicitor may take security from his client for his costs, to be ascertained by taxation or otherwise, in respect of any contentious business to be done by him.

(2) If a solicitor who has been retained by a client to conduct contentious business requests the client to make a payment of a sum of money, being a reasonable sum on account of the costs incurred or to be incurred in the conduct of that business and the client refuses or fails within a reasonable time to make that payment, the refusal or failure shall be deemed to be a good cause whereby the solicitor may, upon giving reasonable notice to the client, withdraw from the retainer.

Section 66 - Taxation with respect to contentious business

Subject to the provisions of any rules of court, on every taxation of costs in respect of any contentious business, the taxing officer may -

(a) allow interest at such rate and from such time as he thinks just on money disbursed by the solicitor for the client, and on money of the client in the hands of, and improperly retained by, the solicitor; and

(b) in determining the remuneration of the solicitor, have regard to the skill, labour and responsibility involved in the business done by him.

Section 67 - Inclusion of disbursements in bill of costs

A solicitor's bill of costs may include costs payable in discharge of a liability properly incurred by him on behalf of the party to be charged with the bill (including counsel's fees) notwithstanding that those costs have not been paid before the delivery of the bill to that party; but those costs -

(a) shall be described in the bill as not then paid; and

(b) if the bill is taxed, shall not be allowed by the taxing officer unless they are paid before the taxation is completed.

Section 68 - Power of Court to order solicitor to deliver bill, etc.

(1) The jurisdiction of the High Court to make orders for the delivery by a solicitor of a bill of costs, and for the delivery up of, or otherwise in relation to, any documents in his possession, custody or power, is hereby declared to extend to cases in which no business has been done by him in the High Court.

(2) A county court shall have the same jurisdiction as the High Court to make orders making such provision as is mentioned in subsection (1) in cases where the bill of costs or the documents relate wholly or partly to contentious business done by the solicitor in that county court.

(3) In this section and in sections 69 to 71 "solicitor" includes the executors, administrators and assignees of a solicitor.

Section 69 - Action to recover solicitor's costs

(1) Subject to the provisions of this Act, no action shall be brought to recover any costs due to a solicitor before the expiration of one month from the date on which a bill of those costs is delivered in accordance with the requirements mentioned in subsection (2); but if there is probable cause for believing that the party chargeable with the costs -

APPENDIX 1

    (a)   is about to quit England and Wales, to become bankrupt or to compound with his creditors, or,

    (b)   is about to do any other act which would tend to prevent or delay the solicitor obtaining payment,

the High Court may, notwithstanding that one month has not expired from the delivery of the bill, order that the solicitor be at liberty to commence an action to recover his costs and may order that those costs be taxed.

(2) The requirements referred to in subsection (1) are that the bill -

    (a)   must be signed by the solicitor, or if the costs are due to a firm, by one of the partners of that firm, either in his own name or in the name of the firm, or be enclosed in, or accompanied by, a letter which is so signed and refers to the bill; and

    (b)   must be delivered to the party to be charged with the bill, either personally or by being sent to him by post to, or left for him at, his place of business, dwelling-house, or last known place of abode;

and, where a bill is proved to have been delivered in compliance with those requirements, it shall not be necessary in the first instance for the solicitor to prove the contents of the bill and it shall be presumed, until the contrary is shown, to be a bill bona fide complying with this Act.

(3) Where a bill of costs relates wholly or partly to contentious business done in a county court and the amount of the bill does not exceed £5,000, the powers and duties of the High Court under this section and sections 70 and 71 in relation to that bill may be exercised and performed by any county court in which any part of the business was done.

(4) [Repealed by S.I. 1991 No 724.]

Section 70 - Taxation on application of party chargeable or solicitor

(1) Where before the expiration of one month from the delivery of a solicitor's bill an application is made by the party chargeable with the bill, the High Court shall, without requiring any sum to be paid into court, order that the bill be taxed and that no action be commenced on the bill until the taxation is completed.

(2) Where no such application is made before the expiration of the period mentioned in subsection (1) then, on an application being made by the solicitor or, subject to subsections (3) and (4) by the party chargeable with the bill, the court may on such terms, if any, as it thinks fit (not being terms as to the costs of the taxation) order -

    (a)   that the bill be taxed; and

(c) that no action be commenced on the bill, and that any action already commenced be stayed, until the taxation is completed.

(3) Where an application under subsection (2) is made by the party chargeable with the bill -

    (a) after the expiration of 12 months from the delivery of the bill, or

    (b) after a judgment has been obtained for the recovery of the costs covered by the bill, or

    (d) after the bill has been paid, but before the expiration of 12 months from the payment of the bill,

no order shall be made except in special circumstances and, if an order is made, it may contain such terms as regards the costs of the taxation as the court may think fit.

(4) The power to order taxation conferred by subsection (2) shall not be exercisable on an application made by the party chargeable with the bill after the expiration of 12 months from the payment of the bill.

(5) An order for the taxation of a bill made on an application under this section by the party chargeable with the bill shall, if he so requests, be an order for the taxation of the profit costs covered by the bill.

(6) Subject to subsection (5) the court may under this section order the taxation of all the costs, or of the profit costs, or of the costs other than profit costs and, where part of the costs is not to be taxed, may allow an action to be commenced or to be continued for that part of the costs.

(7) Every order for the taxation of a bill shall require the taxing officer to tax not only the bill but also the costs of the taxation and to certify what is due to or by the solicitor in respect of the bill and in respect of the costs of the taxation.

(8) If after due notice of any taxation either party to it fails to attend, the officer may proceed with the taxation ex parte.

(9) Unless -

    (a) the order for taxation was made on the application of the solicitor and the party chargeable does not attend the taxation or,

    (b) the order for taxation or an order under subsection (10) otherwise provides,

the costs of a taxation shall be paid according to the event of the taxation, that is to say, if one fifth of the amount of the bill is taxed off, the solicitor shall pay the costs, but otherwise the party chargeable shall pay the costs.

(10) The taxing officer may certify to the court any special circumstances relating to a bill or to the taxation of a bill, and the court may make such order as respects the costs of the taxation as it may think fit.

(11) Subsection (9) shall have effect in any case where the application for an order for taxation was made

APPENDIX 1

before the passing of the Solicitors (Amendment) Act 1974 and -

 (a) the bill is a bill for contentious business, or

 (b) more than half of the amount of the bill before taxation consists of costs for which a scale charge is provided by an order for the time being in operation under section 56,

as if for the reference to one-fifth of the amount of the bill there were substituted a reference to one-sixth of that amount.

(12) In this section "profit costs" means costs other than counsel's fees or costs paid or payable in the discharge of a liability incurred by the solicitor on behalf of the party chargeable, and the reference in subsection (9) to the fraction of the amount of the bill taxed off shall be taken, where the taxation concerns only part of the costs covered by the bill, as a reference to that fraction of the amount of those costs which is being taxed.

Section 71 - Taxation on application of third parties

(1) Where a person other than the party chargeable with the bill for the purposes of section 70 has paid, or is or was liable to pay, a bill either to the solicitor or to the party chargeable with the bill, that person or his executors, administrators or assignees may apply to the High Court for an order for the taxation of the bill as if he were the party chargeable with it, and the court may make the same order (if any) as it might have made if the application had been made by the party chargeable with the bill.

(2) Where the court has no power to make an order by virtue of subsection (1) except in special circumstances it may, in considering whether there are special circumstances sufficient to justify the making of an order, take into account circumstances which affect the applicant but do not affect the party chargeable with the bill.

(3) Where a trustee, executor or administrator has become liable to pay a bill of a solicitor, then, on the application of any person interested in any property out of which the trustee, executor or administrator has paid, or is entitled to pay, the bill, the court may order -

 (a) that the bill be taxed on such terms, if any, as it thinks fit; and

 (c) that such payments, in respect of the amount found to be due to or by a solicitor and in respect of the costs of the taxation, be made to or by the applicant, to or by the solicitor, or to or by the executor, administrator or trustee, as it thinks fit.

(4) In considering any application under subsection (3) the court shall have regard -

 (a) to the provisions of section 70 as to applications by the party chargeable for the taxation of a solicitor's bill so far as they are capable of being applied to an application made under that subsection;

A STRAIGHTFORWARD GUIDE TO YOU AND YOUR SOLICITOR

    (b)   to the extent and nature of the interest of the applicant.

(5) If an applicant under subsection (3) pays any money to the solicitor, he shall have the same right to be paid that money by the trustee, executor or administrator chargeable with the bill as the solicitor had.

(6) Except in special circumstances, no order shall be made on an application under this section for the taxation of a bill which has already been taxed.

(7) If the court on an application under this section orders a bill to be taxed, it may order the solicitor to deliver to the applicant a copy of the bill on payment of the costs of that copy.

Section 72 - Supplementary provisions as to taxations

(1) Every application for an order for the taxation of a solicitor's bill or for the delivery of a solicitor's bill and for the delivery up by a solicitor of any documents in his possession, custody or power shall be made in the matter of that solicitor.

(2) Where a taxing officer is in the course of taxing a bill of costs, he may request the taxing officer of any other court to assist him in taxing any part of the bill, and the taxing officer so requested shall tax that part of the bill and shall return the bill with his opinion on it to the taxing officer making the request.

(3) Where a request is made as mentioned in subsection (2) the taxing officer who is requested to tax part of a bill shall have such powers, and may take such fees, in respect of that part of the bill, as he would have or be entitled to take if he were taxing that part of the bill in pursuance of an order of the court of which he is an officer; and the taxing officer who made the request shall not take any fee in respect of t that part of the bill.

(4) The certificate of the taxing officer by whom any bill has been taxed shall, unless it is set aside or altered by the court, be final as to the amount of the costs covered by it, and the court may make such order in relation to the certificate as it thinks fit, including, in a case where the retainer is not disputed, an order that judgment be entered for the sum certified to be due with costs.

Section 73 - Charging orders

(1) Subject to subsection (2) any court in which a solicitor has been employed to prosecute or defend any suit, matter or proceeding may at any time -

    (a)   declare the solicitor entitled to a charge on any property recovered or preserved through his instrumentality for his taxed costs in relation to that suit, matter or proceeding; and

    (b)   make such orders for the taxation of those costs and for raising money to pay or for paying them out of the property recovered or preserved as the court thinks fit;

and all conveyances and acts done to defeat, or operating to defeat, that charge shall, except in the case of a conveyance to a bona fide purchaser for value without notice, be void as against the solicitor.

APPENDIX 1

(2) No order shall be made under subsection (1) if the right to recover the costs is barred by any statute of limitations.

Section 74 - Special provision as to contentious business done in county courts

(1) The remuneration of a solicitor in respect of contentious business done by him in a county court shall be regulated in accordance with sections 59 to 73, and for that purpose those sections shall have effect subject to the following provisions of this section.

(2) The registrar of a county court shall be the taxing officer of that court but any taxation of costs by him may be reviewed by a judge assigned to the county court district, or by a judge acting as a judge so assigned, on the application of any part to the taxation.

(3) The amount which may be allowed on the taxation of any costs or bill of costs in respect of any item relating to proceedings in a county court shall not, except in so far as rules of court may otherwise provide, exceed the amount which could have been allowed in respect of that item as between party and party in those proceedings, having regard to the nature of the proceedings and the amount of the claim and of any counterclaim.

Section 79(1) - Committees and sub-committees of the Council

(1) Subject to any provision to the contrary made by or under any enactment, the Council may arrange for any of its functions (other than reserved functions) to be discharged by -

    (a) a committee of the Council;

    (b) a sub-committee of such a committee; or

    (c) an individual (whether or not a member of the Society's staff).

    [(2) to (12) not here reproduced.]

Section 81 - Administration of Oaths and Taking of affidavits

(1) Subject to the provisions of this section, every solicitor who holds a practising certificate which is in force shall have the powers conferred on a commissioner for oaths by the Commissioners for Oaths Acts 1889 and 1891 and section 24 of the Stamp Duties Management Act 1891; and any reference to such a commissioner in an enactment or instrument (including an enactment passed or instrument made after the commencement of this Act) shall include a reference to such a solicitor unless the context otherwise requires.

(2) A solicitor shall not exercise the powers conferred by this section in a proceeding in which he is solicitor to any of the parties, or in which he is interested.

(3) A solicitor before whom any oath or affidavit is taken or made shall state in the jurat or attestation at which place and on what date the oath or affidavit is taken or made.

(4) A document containing such a statement and purporting to be sealed or signed by a solicitor shall be

admitted in evidence without proof of the seal or signature, and without proof that he is a solicitor or that he holds a practising certificate which is in force.

Section 87 - Interpretation

(1) "contentious business" means business done, whether as solicitor or advocate, in or for the purposes of proceedings begun before a court or before an arbitrator appointed under the Arbitration Act 1950, not being business which falls within the definition of non-contentious or common form probate business contained in section 128 of the Supreme Court Act 1981;

"non-contentious business" means any business done as a solicitor which is not contentious business as defined by this subsection.

Schedule 1A - INADEQUATE PROFESSIONAL SERVICES

Circumstances in which Council's powers may be exercised

1.-(1) The Council may take any of the steps mentioned in paragraph 2 ("the steps") with respect to a solicitor where it appears to them that the professional services provided by him in connection with any matter in which he or his firm have been instructed by a client have, in any respect, not been of the quality which it is reasonable to expect of him as a solicitor.

(2) The Council shall not take any steps unless they are satisfied that in all the circumstances of the case it is appropriate to do so.

(3) In determining in any case whether it is appropriate to take any of the steps, the Council may -

    (a) have regard to the existence of any remedy which it is reasonable to expect to be available to the client in civil proceedings; and

    (b) where proceedings seeking any such remedy have not been begun by him, have regard to whether it is reasonable to expect him to begin them.

Directions which may be given

2.-(1) The steps are -

    (a) determining that the costs to which the solicitor is entitled in respect of his services ("the costs") are to be limited to such amount as may be specified in the determination and directing him to comply, or to secure compliance, with such one or more of the permitted requirements as appear to the Council to be necessary in order for effect to be given to their determination;

    (b) directing him to secure the rectification, at his expense or that of his firm, of any such error, omission or other deficiency arising in connection with the matter in question as they may specify;

(c) directing him to pay such compensation to the client as the Council sees fit to specify in the direction;

(d) directing him to take, at his expense or at that of his firm, such other action in the interests of the client as they may specify.

(2) The "permitted requirements" are -

(a) that the whole or part of any amount already paid by or on behalf of the client in respect of the costs be refunded;

(b) that the whole part of the costs be remitted;

(c) that the right to recover the costs be waived, whether wholly or to any specified extent.

(3) The power of the Council to take any such steps is not confined to cases where the client may have a cause of action against the solicitor for negligence.

Compensation

3.-(1) The amount [presently] specified in a direction by virtue of paragraph 2(1)(c) shall not exceed £1,000.

(2) The Lord Chancellor may by order made by statutory instrument amend sub-paragraph (1) by substituting for the sum of £1,000 such other sum as he considers appropriate.

(3) Before making any such order the Lord Chancellor shall consult the Law Society.

(4) Any statutory instrument made under this paragraph shall be subject to annulment in pursuance of a resolution of either House of Parliament.

[4. Taxation of costs	*Not here reproduced]*
[5 Failure to comply with direction	*Not here reproduced]*
[6 Fees	*Not here reproduced]*
[7 Costs	*Not here reproduced]*
[8 Duty of tribunal	*Not here reproduced]*
[9 Interpretation	*Not here reproduced]*

APPENDIX 2

SOLICITORS' ACCOUNTS RULES 1991
(with consolidated amendments to 1 June 1992)

Rules dated 16th July 1991 made by the Council of the Law Society and approved by the Master of the Rolls pursuant to section 32 of the Solicitors Act 1974 and section 9 of the Administration of Justice Act 1985 regulating the keeping of accounts by solicitors, registered foreign lawyers and recognised bodies in respect of their English and Welsh practices.

Commencement and interpretation

1. These rules may be cited as the Solicitors' Accounts Rules 1991 and shall come into operation on the 1st day of June 1992 whereupon the Solicitors' Accounts Rules 1986, the Solicitors' Trust Accounts Rules 1986 and the Solicitors' Accounts (Deposit Interest) Rules 1988 shall cease to have effect.

2. (1) In these Rules, unless the context otherwise requires -

>the expression "accounts", "books", "ledgers" and "records" shall be deemed to include loose-leaf books and such cards or other permanent documents or records as are necessary for the operation of any system of book-keeping, computerised, mechanical or otherwise and where a computerised system is operated, the information recorded on it must be capable of being reproduced in hard printed form within a reasonable time;

>"bank" shall mean the branch, situated in England or Wales, of a bank as defined by section 87(1) of the Solicitors Act 1974, as amended by paragraph 9 of Schedule 6 to the Banking Act 1979 and paragraph 5 of Schedule 6 to the Banking Act 1987;

>"building society" shall mean the branch, situated in England or Wales, of a building society as defined by paragraph 11(5) of Schedule 18 to the Building Societies Act 1986;

>"client", save in Part III of these rules, shall mean any person on whose account a solicitor holds or receives client's money;

>"client account" shall mean a current or deposit account at a bank or deposit account with a building society in the name of the solicitor or his or her firm in the title of which account the word "client" appears;

>"client's money" shall mean money held or received by a solicitor on account of a person for whom he or she is acting in relation to the holding or receipt of such money either as a solicitor or, in connection with his or her practice as a solicitor, as agent, bailee, stakeholder or in any other capacity; provided that the expression "client's money" shall not include -

APPENDIX 2

(a) money held or received on account of the trustees of a trust of which the solicitor is a controlled trustee; or

(b) money to which the only person entitled is the solicitor himself or herself or, in the case of a firm of solicitors, one or more of the partners in the firm;

"controlled trust" in relation to a solicitor, shall mean a trust of which he or she is a controlled trustee;

"controlled trust account" shall mean a current or deposit account kept at a bank or deposit account kept with a building society in the title of which the word "trustee" or "executor" appears, or which is otherwise clearly designated as a controlled trust account, and kept solely for money subject to a particular trust of which the solicitor is a controlled trustee;

"controlled trustee" shall mean a solicitor who is a sole trustee or co-trustee only with one or more of his of her partners or employees and any reference to a controlled trustee shall be construed as including -

(a) a recognised body which is a sole trustee or co-trustee only with one or more of its officers, partners or employees; and

(b) a solicitor or a recognised body who or which is an officer or employee of a recognised body and who or which is a sole trustee or co-trustee only with one or more other officers or employees of that recognised body or the body itself;

"costs" includes fees, charges, disbursements, expenses and remuneration and, for the purpose of rules 7(a)(iv) and 9(2)(c)(i), shall include costs (including VAT) in respect of which a solicitor has incurred a liability but shall exclude the fees of counsel or other lawyer, or of a professional or other agent, or of an expert instructed by the solicitor;

"local authority" shall have the same meaning as is given to this expression by the Local Government Act 1972;

"private loan" shall mean a loan other than one provided by an institution which provides loans in the normal course of its activities;

"public officer" shall mean an officer whose remuneration is defrayed out of moneys provided by Parliament, the revenues of the Duchy of Cornwall or the Duchy of Lancaster, the general fund of the Church Commissioners, the Forestry Fund or the Development Fund;

"recognised body" shall have the meaning assigned to it by the Solicitors' Incorporated Practice Rules 1988 as may be amended, modified or re-enacted from time to time;

"separate designated account" shall mean a deposit account at a bank or building society in the name of the solicitor or his or her firm in the title of which account the word "client" appears and which is designated by reference to the identity of the client or matter concerned;

"solicitor" shall mean a solicitor of the Supreme Court and shall include a firm of solicitors or a recognised body;

"trust money" shall mean money held or received by a solicitor which is not client's money and which is subject to a trust of which the solicitor is a trustee whether or not he or she is a controlled trustee of such trust;

words in the singular include the plural, words in the plural include the singular and words importing the masculine or feminine shall include the neuter; and

(3) Other expressions in these rules shall except where otherwise stated have the meanings assigned to them by the Solicitors Act 1974.

Part I - General

2. Subject to the provisions of rule 9 hereof, every solicitor who holds or receives client's money, or money which under rule 4 hereof the solicitor is permitted and elects to pay into a client account, shall without delay pay such money into a client account. Any solicitor may keep one client account or as many such accounts as the solicitor thinks fit.

4. There may be paid into a client account -

    (a) trust money;

    (c) such money belonging to the solicitor as may be necessary for the purpose of opening or maintaining the account;

    (d) money to replace any sum which for any reason may have been drawn from the account in contravention of paragraph (2) of rule 8 of these rules; and

    (e) money received by the solicitor which under paragraph (b) of rule 5 of these rules the solicitor is entitled to split but which the solicitor does not split.

5. Where a solicitor holds or receives money which includes client's money or trust money of one or more trusts -

    (a) he or she may where practicable split such money and, if he or she does so, he or she shall deal with each part thereof as if he or she had received a separate sum of money in respect of that part; or

    (b) if he or she does not split the money he or she shall, if any part thereof consists of client's money, and may, in any other case, pay the money into a client account.

5A. When a solicitor received, in full or part settlement of a bill of costs, a payment all of which is money to which the solicitor alone is entitled, the solicitor may, as an alternative to treating the money in accordance with rule 9(2), elect to pay it without delay into a client account provided that the money does not remain in a client account longer than seven days from receipt.

APPENDIX 2

6. No money other than money which under the foregoing rules a solicitor is required or permitted to pay into a client account shall be paid into a client account, and it shall be the duty of a solicitor into whose client account any money has been paid in contravention of this rule to withdraw the same without delay on discovery.

7. There may be drawn from a client account -

    (a) in the case of client's money -

        (i) money properly required for a payment to or on behalf of the client;

        (ii) money properly required in full or partial reimbursement of money expended by the solicitor on behalf of the client;

        (iii) money drawn on the client's authority;

        (iv) money properly required for or towards payment of the solicitor's costs where there has been delivered to the client a bill of costs or other written intimation of the amount of the costs incurred and it has thereby or otherwise in writing been made clear to the client that money held for him or her is being or will be applied towards or in satisfaction of such costs; and

        (v) money which is transferred into another client account;

    (b) in the case of trust money -

        (i) money properly required for a payment in the execution of the particular trust, and

        (ii) money to be transferred to a separate bank or building society account kept solely for the money of the particular trust;

    (c) money, not being money to which either paragraph (a) or paragraph (b) of this rule applies, as may have been paid into the account under rule 4(b) or rule 5(b) or rule 5A of these rules;

    (d) money which for any reason may have been paid into the account in contravention of rule 6 of these rules;

    provided that in any case under paragraph (a) and paragraph (b) of this rule the money so drawn shall not exceed the total of the money held for the time being in such account on account of such client or trust.

8. (1) No money drawn from a client account under sub-paragraph (ii) or sub-paragraph (iv) of paragraph (a) or under paragraph (c) or paragraph (d) of rule 7 of these rules shall be drawn up except by -

    (a) a cheque drawn in favour of the solicitor, or

    (b) transfer to a bank or building society account in the name of the solicitor not being a client account.

A STRAIGHTFORWARD GUIDE TO YOU AND YOUR SOLICITOR

(2) No money other than money permitted by rule 7 to be drawn from a client account shall be so drawn unless the Council upon an application made to them by the solicitor specifically authorise in writing its withdrawal.

9. (1) Notwithstanding the provisions of these rules, a solicitor shall not be under an obligation to pay into a client account client's money held or received by him or her -

   (a) which is received by him or her in the form of cash and is without delay paid in cash in the ordinary course of business to the client or on his or her behalf to a third party; or

   (b) which is received by him or her in the form of a cheque or draft which is endorsed over the ordinary course of business to the client or on his or her behalf to a third party and is not passed by the solicitor through a bank or building society account; or

   (c) which he or she pays into a separate bank or building society account opened or to be opened in the name of the client or of some person designated by the client in writing or acknowledged by the solicitor to the client in writing.

   (2) Notwithstanding the provision of these rules (and except where the solicitor elects to treat a payment in accordance with rule 5A and complies with the requirements of that rule), a solicitor shall not pay into a client account money held or received by him or her -

   (a) which the client for his or her own convenience requests the solicitor to withhold from such account, such request being either in writing from the client or acknowledged by the solicitor to the client in writing; or

   (b) which is received by him or her from the client in full or partial reimbursement of money expended by the solicitor on behalf of the client; or

   (c) which is expressly paid to him or her either -

       (i) for or towards payment of the solicitor's costs in respect of which a bill of costs or other written intimation of the amount of the costs incurred has been delivered for payment; or

       (ii) as an agreed fee (or on account of an agreed fee) for business undertaken or to be undertaken.

   (3) Where money includes client's money as well as money of the nature described in paragraph (2) of these rule such money shall be dealt with in accordance with rule 5 of these rules.

   (4) Notwithstanding the provisions of these rules the Council may upon application made to them by a solicitor specifically authorise such solicitor in writing to withhold any client's money from a client account.

10. (1) No sum shall be transferred from the ledger account of one client to that of another except in circumstances in which it would have been permissible under these rules to have withdrawn from

client account the sum transferred from the first client and to have paid into client account the sum so transferred to the second client.

(2) No sum in respect of provide loan shall be paid -

    (a)   directly; or

    (b)   by means of a transfer from the ledger account of one client to that of another;
out of funds held on account of the lender without the prior written authority of the lender.

11. (1) Every solicitor shall at all times keep properly written up such accounts as may be necessary -

    (a)   to show the solicitor's dealings with -

        (i)   client's money received, held or paid by him or her; and

        (ii)   any other money dealt with by him or her through a client account; and

    (b)   (i)   subject to rule 11(3) below to show separately in respect of each client all money of the categories specified in sub-paragraph (a) of this paragraph which is received, held or paid by him or her on account of that client; and

        (ii)   to distinguish all money of the said categories received, held or paid by him or her, from any other money received, held or paid by him or her; and

    (c)   to show the current balance on each client's ledger.

(2)(a) All dealings referred to in sub-paragraph (a) of paragraph (1) of this rule shall be appropriately recorded -

        (i)   in a clients' cash account; or a clients' column of a cash account or in a record of sums transferred from the ledger account of one client to that of another; and

        (ii)   in a clients' ledger or a clients' column of a ledger, and no other dealings shall be recorded in such clients' cash account, ledger, record of sums transferred or, as the case may be, in such clients' columns.

    (b)   All dealings of the solicitor relating to his or her practice as a solicitor other than those referred to in sub-paragraph (a) of paragraph (1) of this rule shall (subject to compliance with Part II of these rules) be recorded in a separate cash account and ledger or such other columns of a cash account and ledger as the solicitor may maintain.

(3) A solicitor acting for both borrower and lender in a conveyancing transaction who received from the lender a mortgage advance shall not be required to open separate ledger accounts for both borrower and lender in respect of such advance provided that -

    (a)   the funds belonging to each client are clearly identifiable; and

A STRAIGHTFORWARD GUIDE TO YOU AND YOUR SOLICITOR

    (b)   the lender is the institutional lender which provides mortgages in the normal course of its activities.

(4)   In addition to the books, ledgers and records referred to in paragraph (2) of this rule, every solicitor shall keep a record of all bills of costs (distinguishing between profit costs and disbursements) and of all written intimations under rule 7(a)(iv) and under rule 9(2)(c) of these rules delivered or made by the solicitor to his or her clients, which record shall be contained in a bills delivered book or a file of copies of such bills and intimations.

(5)   Every solicitor shall, at least once every five weeks -

    (i)   compare the total of the balances shown by the clients' ledger accounts of the liabilities to the clients, including those for whom trust money is held in the client account, with the cash account balance; and

    (ii)   prepare a reconciliation statement showing the cause of the difference, if any, shown by the above comparison; and

    (iii)   reconcile that cash account balance with the balances shown on client account bank and building society pass books or statements and money held elsewhere;

and shall preserve the records of all such reconciliations.

(6)   A withdrawal from a bank or building society account, being or forming part of a client account, may only be made where a specific authority in respect of that withdrawal has been signed by one at least of the following (either alone or in conjunction with other persons) namely -

    (i)   a solicitor who holds a current practising certificate; or

    (ii)   an employee of such a solicitor being either a solicitor or a Fellow of the Institute of Legal Executives who is confirmed by the Institute as being of good standing and who shall have been admitted a Fellow for not less than three years;

    (iia)   a registered foreign lawyer who is a partner or director of the practice;

    (iii)   in the case of an office dealing solely with conveyancing, an employee of such a solicitor being a licensed conveyancer.

(7)   Rule 11(6) shall not apply to the transfer of money from one account to another at the same bank or building society where both accounts are client accounts other than separate designated accounts.

(8)   For the purpose of rule 11(6) of these rules the first and third references to a solicitor shall not be construed as including references to a recognised body and the references to an employee of 'such a solicitor' shall be construed as including a reference to an employee of a recognised body.

(9)(a)   Every solicitor shall preserve for at least six years -

    (i)   from the date of the last entry therein all accounts, books, ledgers and records; and

APPENDIX 2

    (ii) all bank statements as printed and issued by the bank.

(b) Every solicitor shall retain for at least two years -

    (i) all paid cheques unless he or she has arranged in writing with the relevant bank(s) and/or building society(ies) that they will retain such paid cheques for that period; and

    (ii) copies of the authorities (other than cheques) signed pursuant to rule 11(6).

(10) This rule 11 shall apply only to Part I of these rules.

Part II - Controlled Trusts

12. Subject to the provisions of rule 18 of these rules every controlled trustee who holds or receives money subject to a trust of which he or she is a controlled trustee, other than money which is paid into a client account as permitted by Part I of these rules, shall without delay pay such money into a controlled trust account of the particular trust.

13. There may be paid into a controlled trust account -

  (a) money subject to the particular trust;

  (b) such money belonging to the controlled trustee or to a co-trustee as may be necessary for the purpose of opening or maintaining the account; and

  (c) money to replace any sum which for any reason may have been drawn from the account in contravention of rule 17 of these rules.

13. Where a solicitor holds or receives money which includes money subject to a trust or trusts of which the solicitor is controlled trustee -

  (a) he or she shall where practicable split such money and, if he or she does so, shall deal with each part thereof as if he or she had received a separate sum of money in respect of that part; or

  (b) if he or she does not split the money, he or she may pay it into a client account as permitted by Part I of these rules.

14. No money, other than money which under rules 12 to 14 of these rules a solicitor is required or permitted to pay into a controlled trust account, shall be paid into a controlled trust account, and it shall be the duty of a solicitor into whose controlled trust account any money has been paid in contravention of this rule to withdraw the same without delay on discovery.

16. There may be drawn from a controlled trust account -

  (a) money properly required for a payment in the execution of the particular trust;

(b) money to be transferred to a client account;

(c) such money, not being money subject to the particular trust, as may have been paid into the account under paragraph (b) of rule 13 of these rules; or

(d) money which may for any reason have been paid into the account in contravention of rule 15 of these rules.

17. No money other than money permitted by rule 16 of these rules to be drawn from a controlled trust account shall be so drawn unless the Council upon an application made to them by the solicitor expressly authorise in writing its withdrawal.

18. Notwithstanding the provisions of these rules a solicitor shall not be under an obligation to pay into a controlled trust account money held or received by him or her which is subject to a trust of which he or she is controlled trustee -

    (a) if the money is received by him or her in the form of cash and is without delay paid in cash in the execution of the trust to a third party; or

    (b) if the money is received by him or her in the form of a cheque or draft which is without delay endorsed over in the execution of the trust to a third party and is not passed by the solicitor through a bank or building society account.

19. Except in so far as money is dealt with in accordance with Part I of these rules -

    (a) every controlled trustee shall at all times keep properly written up such accounts as may be necessary -

        (i) to show separately in respect of each trust of which he or she is a controlled trustee all his or her dealings with money received, held or paid by him or her on account of that trust; and

        (ii) to distinguish the same from money received held or paid by him or her on any other account;

    (b) every controlled trustee shall preserve for at least six years from the date of the last entry therein all accounts and bank statements;

    (c) every controlled trustee shall either -

        (i) keep together, centrally, the accounts which he or she is required to keep under this rule 19; or

        (ii) maintain centrally a register of the trusts in respect of which he or she is required to keep accounts under this rule 19.

APPENDIX 2

Part III - Interest

20 (1) Subject to rule 26 of these rules, a solicitor who holds money for or on account of a client shall account to the client for interest or an equivalent sum in the following circumstances:

    (i) where such money is held on deposit in a separate designated account the solicitor shall account to the client for the interest earned on that money;

    (ii) where such money is not so held on deposit, the solicitor shall, subject to rule 21 of these rules pay to the client out of the solicitor's own money a sum equivalent to the interest which would have accrued if the money received had been so kept on deposit, or its gross equivalent if the interest would have been net of tax.

(2) In paragraph (1) of this rule, for the avoidance of doubt, the reference to a solicitor who holds money for or on account of a client includes the solicitor holding money in his or her capacity as solicitor on account of the trustees of a trust (other than a controlled trust) of which the solicitor is a trustee.

21. A solicitor shall only be required to account in accordance with rule 20(1)(ii) of these rules where:

    (i) the solicitor holds the money for as long as or longer than the number of weeks set out in the left hand column of the table below and the minimum amount held equals or exceeds the corresponding figure in the right hand column of the table:

Table

No. of weeks	Minimum amount
8	£1,000
4	£2,000
2	£10,000
1	£20,000

or

    (ii) the solicitor holds a sum of money exceeding £20,000 for less than one week and it is fair and reasonable to so account having regard to all the circumstances; or

    (iii) the solicitor holds money continuously which varies significantly in amount over the period during which it is held and it is fair and reasonable so to account having regard to any sum payable under paragraph (i) of this rule and to the varying amounts of money and length of time for which these rules are held; or

    (iv) the solicitor holds sums of money intermittently during the course of acting and it is fair and reasonable so to account having regard to all the circumstances including the aggregate of the sums held and the periods for which they are held notwithstanding that no individual sum would have attracted interest under paragraph (i) of this rule; or

    (v)   rule 22 of these rules applies.

22. Where money is held by a solicitor for or on account of a client for a continuous period and the money is held on deposit in a separate designated account for only part of that period, and no interest would be payable for the rest of the period under rule 21(i) to (iii) of these rules, the solicitor shall:

    (i)   for the part of the period during which the money was so held on deposit, account for interest in accordance with rule 20(1)(i) of these rules; and

    (ii)   for the rest of the period, pay interest where it is fair and reasonable to do so having regard to all the circumstances including the interest which would have been payable under rule 21(i) to (iii) if the money had been kept off deposit for the whole of the period.

23. For the purposes of rule 20(1)(ii) of these rules the sum payable to the client shall be calculated by reference to the interest payable on a separate designated account:

    (i)   at the bank or building society where the money is held; or

    (ii)   where the money, or part of it, is held in successive and concurrent accounts maintained at different banks or building societies, at whichever of those banks or building societies was offering the highest rate of interest on such account on the day when the sum payable under rule 20(1)(ii) commenced to accrue; or

    (iii)   where, contrary to the provisions of Parts I and II of these rules, the money is not held in a client account, at any bank or building society nominated by the client.

24. Subject to rule 26(c) of these rules, where a solicitor holds money as a stakeholders (whether or not such money is paid by a client of the solicitor) the solicitor shall pay interest in accordance with Part III of these rules save that such interest shall be paid to the person to whom the stake is paid.

25. Without prejudice to any other remedy which may be available to him or her, any client who feels aggrieved that interest or a sum equivalent thereto has not been paid to him or her under Part III of these rules shall be entitled to apply to the Law Society for a certificate as to whether or not interest ought to have been earned for him or her and, if so, the amount of such interest: and upon the issue of such a certificate the sum certified to be due shall be payable by the solicitor to the client.

26. Nothing in Part III of these rules shall:

    (a)   affect any arrangement in writing, whenever made, between a solicitor and his or her client as to the application of the client's money or interest thereon;

    (b)   apply to money received by a solicitor:

(i) being money subject to a controlled trust; or

(ii) in his or her capacity as trustee rather than as solicitor, on account of the trustees of any other trust of which the solicitor is a trustee;

(b) affect any agreement in writing for payment of interest on stakeholder money held by a solicitor.

[Part IV - Compliance omitted.]
[Part V - Application omitted.]

APPENDIX 3

ORDER 106 Amended pursuant to S.I.1998 3132 (L17)

Rule 2 - Jurisdiction under Part III of Act

(1) Deleted

(2) The jurisdiction of the High Court under Part III of the Act may be exercised by -

    (a) a judge sitting in private,

    (b) a master, a taxing master or a district judge of the Family Division, or

    (c) a district judge, if the costs are for contentious business done in proceedings in the district registry of which he is the district judge or for non-contentious business.

Rule 3 - Power to order solicitor to deliver cash account, etc.

(1) Where the relationship of solicitor and client exists or has existed the Court may, on the application of the client or his personal representatives, make an order for -

    (a) the delivery by the solicitor of a cash account;

    (b) the payment or delivery up by the solicitor of money or securities;

    (c) the delivery to the claimant of a list of the moneys or securities which the solicitor has in his possession or control on behalf of the claimant;

    (d) the payment into or lodging in court of any such moneys or securities.

(2) An application for an order under this rule must be made by the issue of a claim form or if in proceedings by an application in accordance with CPR Part 23.

(3) If the defendant alleges that he has a claim for costs, the Court may make such order for the detailed assessment in accordance with CPR 47 and payment, or securing the payment, thereof and the protection of the defendant's lien, if any, as the Court thinks fit.

Rule 5A - Certificate to be submitted with solicitor's application for detailed assessment

A solicitor who applies for an order under the Act for the detailed assessment in accordance with CPR Part 47 of his bill of costs shall lodge with his application a certificate that all the relevant requirements of the Act have been satisfied.

Rule 6 - Applications under Schedule 1 to Act

(1) Proceedings in the High Court under Schedule 1 to the Act shall be assigned to the Chancery Division.

APPENDIX 3

(2) The claim form by which an application for an order under the said Schedule is made must be entitled in the matter of a solicitor, or a deceased solicitor, as the case may be (without naming him) and in the matter of the Act.

(3) Where an order has been made under paragraph 9(4), 9(5) or 10 of the said Schedule an application for an order under paragraph 9(8) or 9(10) may be made in accordance with CPR Part 23 in the proceedings in which the first mentioned order was made.

Rule 7 - Defendants to applications under Schedule 1 to Act

The defendant to a claim by which an application for an order under Schedule 1 to the Act is made shall be -

(a) if the application is for an order under paragraph 5 thereof, the solicitor or, as the case may be, every member of the firm, on whose behalf the money in respect of which the order is sought is held;

(b) if the application is for an order under paragraph 6(4) or 9(8) thereof, the Law Society;

(b) if the application is for an order under paragraph 8, 9(4) or 9(5) thereof, the person against whom the order is sought;

(c) if the application is for an order under paragraph 9(10) thereof, the person from whom the Law Society obtained possession of the documents by virtue of paragraph 9 or 10;

(d) if the application is for an order under paragraph 10 thereof for the re-direction of postal packets addressed to a solicitor or his firm, the solicitor or, as the case may be, every member of the firm;

(e) if the application is for an order under paragraph 11 thereof, the solicitor or personal representative in substitution for whom the appointment of a new trustee is sought and, if he is a co-trustee, the other trustee or trustees.

Rule 8 - Interim order restricting payment out of banking account

At any time after the issue of a claim by which an application for an order under paragraph 5 of Schedule 1 to the Act is made, the Court may, on the application of the claimant made without notice in accordance with CPR Part 23 make an interim order under that paragraph to have effect until the hearing of the application and include therein a further order requiring the defendant to show cause at the hearing why an order under that paragraph should not be made.

Rule 9 - Adding parties, etc.

The Court may, at any stage of proceedings under Schedule 1 to the Act, order any person to be added as a party to the proceedings or to be given notice thereof.

Rule 10 - Service of documents

(1) Any document required to be served on the Law Society in proceedings under this Order shall be

served by sending it by prepaid post to the secretary of the Law Society.

(2) Subject to paragraph (1) a claim form by which an application under Schedule 1 to the Act is made, an order under paragraph 5 of that Schedule or rule 8 and any other document not required to be served personally which is to be served on a defendant to proceedings under the said Schedule shall, unless the Court otherwise directs, be deemed to be properly served by sending it by prepaid post to the defendant at his last known address.

Rule 11 - Constitution of Division Court to hear appeals

Every appeal shall be heard by a Divisional Court of the Queen's Bench Division consisting, unless the Lord Chief Justice otherwise directs, of not less than three judges.

Rule 14 - Restriction on requiring security for costs

No person other than an appellant who was the applicant in the proceedings before the Tribunal, shall be ordered to give security for the costs of an appeal.

Rule 15 - Disciplinary committee's opinion may be required

The Court may direct the Tribunal to furnish the Court with a written statement of their opinion on the case which is the subject-matter of an appeal or on any question arising therein, and where such a direction is given, the clerk to the Tribunal must as soon as may be lodge three copies of such statement in the Crown Office and at the same time send a copy to each of the parties to the appeal.

APPENDIX 4

[In the High Court of Justice
Queen's Bench Division or
In the   County Court]

[1999-S-No- or
Claim No   ]

Between:-

VIC SEIXAS Claimant
v
EMM BEZELL & LAWLESS (a firm) Defendants

Statement of Case

(a)   The Claimant's claim is for damages for breach of contract and/or professional negligence.

(b)   The Claimant expects to recover more than £15,000 [but cannot say how much he expects to recover]

(c)   The Claimant believes the facts in his statement of case are true.

Particulars of Claim

1. The Defendants are a firm of solicitors and were at all material times practising under the name and style of Emm Bezell and Lawless at 1 Devil's Way Hades Island Essex.

2. On or about 17 March 1996 the Claimant consulted the Defendants at their said offices for professional advice concerning his claims against Hugo Theyer and Yewell Tripp for damages for personal injuries arising from an accident on 1 April 1992.

3. In reliance on the professional expertise of the Defendants, the Claimant retained and employed them as their solicitors for reward and entrusted them with the task of commencing proceedings to recover damages for their claim aforesaid.

4. In the premises it was an implied term of the said contract that the Defendants would exercise due skill and care and observe the time limits laid down by the County Court Rules 1981 save and insofar as the said time limits were extended by order of the court or consent of the Defendants to the claim.

5. Negligently and/or in breach of the said implied terms the Defendants failed to take any or any sufficient action whereby the said claim was automatically struck out on [4 May 1998] pursuant to Order 17 rule 11(9) of the County Court Rules aforesaid.

Particulars

Causing or permitting the Claimant's claim to be automatically struck out by not applying to the court to have the case set down pursuant to the [automatic directions/order therefor dated 4 January 1998] or not applying for an extension of the time limited by the said order.

A STRAIGHTFORWARD GUIDE TO YOU AND YOUR SOLICITOR

6. By virtue of the Defendants' said omissions [and/or the fact that the claim was statute barred because his cause of action arose on 1 April 1992] the Claimant lost his chance of recovering damages in respect of his claim and has thereby suffered loss and damage.

Particulars

(a) The value of the said claim for personal injuries comprising

    (i) General damages for pain, suffering and loss of amenities   £10,000

    (ii) Loss of earnings from 1 April 1992 until [date when he was able to resume work/find suitable alternative employment] at £ a month for months   £30,000

    (iii) Interest at the rate of 8% on the sum of £ , being for [number of months] [from [date] to[date] when he was able to resume,etc.

    (iv) Loss of pension

    (v) [List other types of special damages] e.g. taxis, cleaners, etc.]

(b) Legal costs paid on account to the Defendants   £2,000

(c) Costs paid pursuant to the striking out of the said claim to

    (i) Timus Lee & Co, solicitors for Hugo Theyer aforesaid   £1,800.00

    (ii) Sharks, solicitors for Yewell Tripp aforesaid   <u>£7,500</u>

                         £ 9,300.00

7. Further, pursuant to [Section 35A of the Supreme Courts Act 1981 or Section 69 of the County Courts Act 1984], the Claimant is entitled to and claims to recover interest on the amount found to be due at such rate and for such period as the court may see fit.

And the Claimant claims:
(1) Damages; and
(2) Interest pursuant to [Section 35A of the Supreme Courts Act 1981 or Section 69 of the County Courts Act 1984] aforesaid.